Discovering Literature Series

CHALLENGING LEVEL

D0572303

The Giver

A Teaching Guide

by Mary Elizabeth Podhaizer

Illustrations by Kathy Kifer

Community Strand

Dedicated to
to Brian

The Giver
Published by:
Houghton Mifflin Company
215 Park Avenue South
New York, New York 10003

Teaching Guide Published by:
Garlic Press
1312 Jeppesen Avenue
Eugene, OR 97402

www.garlicpress.com

ISBN 0-931993-97-0
Order Number GP-097
Printed in China

Table of Contents

Table of Contents, Cont.

NOTES TO THE TEACHER

The Discovering Literature Series is designed to develop a student's appreciation for good literature and to improve reading comprehension. At the Challenging Level, we focus on a variety of reading strategies that can help students construct meaning from their experience with literature as well as make connections between their reading and the rest of their lives. The strategies reflect the demands of each literature selection. In this study guide, we will focus on beginning a book, setting and mood, irony, plot structure, foreshadowing and flashback, characterization, forming hypotheses, evaluating a book, plot conflict, point of view, inferencing, rereading, theme, narration, and the genre of dystopias.

ORGANIZATION OF THIS LITERATURE GUIDE

The following discussion explains the various elements that structure the series at the Challenging Level.

Each chapter analysis is organized into three basic elements: **Journal and Discussion Topics, Chapter Vocabulary,** and **Chapter Summary.** One or more of the Journal and Discussion Topics and all of the Chapter Vocabulary can either be displayed on the board or on an overhead projector before each chapter is read. The selected Journal and Discussion Topics will help to focus the students' reading of the chapter. Choose questions that will not give away important plot elements. Introducing the Chapter Vocabulary prior to students' reading insures that their reading is not disrupted by the frequent need to look up a word. Guide students in using one of the vocabulary exercises from page 6 to preview the chapter vocabulary.

Journal and Discussion Topics

The **Journal and Discussion Topics** include questions for the students' Reader Response Journals and questions for Discussion to help the students become engaged with the literature. Students will benefit by reading with their journals beside them. This will allow them to easily note any unfamiliar vocabulary that was not presented to the class, questions they have about the literature, and their own reactions as they enter into the experience of the story. Journals can also be used for written dialogue between you and students. You may wish to periodically collect the journals and respond to students' comments. It is important for students to know beforehand whether their journals are private or public. In either case, journals should not be corrected or graded, but only recorded as being used. You may also wish to keep your own journal.

Discussion can take place between partners, in small groups, or as a whole class. Students may also wish to reflect on the discussion in their journals. Discussion starters include

1. A group retelling of the chapter in which everyone participates.
2. Each group member telling
   a. the most striking moment in the chapter for him or her;
   b. a question she or he would like to ask the author or a character about the chapter; or
   c. what he or she liked most or least about the chapter.

3. A discussion of how the chapter relates to the rest of the book that preceded it.

Discussion may end with predictions about what will happen in the next chapter. Each student should note predictions in her or his journal.

Always ask students to retell (or summarize) the material. The retelling can be oral, artistic (for example, a storyboard), or prose. Retelling can take place in the discussion groups or in the journals.

Chapter Vocabulary

The **Chapter Vocabulary** includes definitions of key words from each chapter. To save time, students need only to copy, not look up, definitions. The more meaningful vocabulary exercises are, the more easily students will retain vocabulary. Suggestions for teaching vocabulary follow.

1. Finding relationships between and among words helps students learn the words better than treating them separately. Have students create a web or other graphic showing the relationships between and among the vocabulary words. Encourage them to add other related words to their web.
2. A group of words that primarily includes nouns can be used to label a picture.
3. Have students use the words in a piece of writing; for example, a poem, a one-act play, a diary entry written from the point of view of one of the characters.
4. Have students research the etymology of each word and keep notes on it.
5. Have students make and exchange crossword puzzles made with the vocabulary words.
6. Have students write and exchange a cloze exercise using the vocabulary words. A cloze exercise has a blank for each vocabulary word, and the surrounding context must clearly indicate which word belongs in each blank.

Chapter Summary

The **Chapter Summary** for each chapter is included for teacher use. It provides an at-a-glance scan of the chapter events. Use it to refresh your memory about the contents of each chapter.

The Groupings of Literature

We have among our titles a group of works that could be part of a unit called "Community." We present literature so that you can easily introduce works as a unit. The works of literature in the "Community" unit resonate with one another, providing a multi-faceted look at a variety of **themes** such as

- Control
- The individual and the system
- Ownership
- Responsibility
- Freedom
- Choices
- Belonging
- Diversity and unity
- Identity
- The ideal society

Since no substantial work of literature has only a single theme, "Community" is not the only possible grouping for these works of literature. But reference to themes can both help focus students' attention as they read and help link works of literature together in meaningful ways. In a similar way, a grouping of books can throw light on **Big Ideas.** Big Ideas worth considering include the following.

- What makes a community?
- How is our community important in our lives?
- How can we contribute to our community?
- How does the community context (cultural, social, etc.) affect individuals?
- How can individual and community goals conflict or coexist?

OTHER FEATURES OF THE CHALLENGING LEVEL

Strategy Pages

Strategy Pages throughout the series have been developed to increase students' understanding of strategies they can use to enhance their understanding of literature. Some important examples are

- Monitoring (such as adjusting reading rate, consulting outside sources for further information, using context, rereading)
- Identifying important information (such as marking a text)
- Summarizing
- Evaluating
- Understanding the tools that writers' use to make meaning—the elements of literature such as theme, plot, character, allusion, etc.

The pages for each literature selection reinforce the strategies important for engaging deeply with that particular work of literature. You may copy and distribute these pages. Students may answer on the back of the page or on a separate sheet of paper. Some questions may require that students read farther before answering. Some require that they reflect on their own experience and knowledge.

Testing

At the end of each chapter grouping, a comprehensive open-book **Test** has been provided for your use. Each test includes vocabulary exercises and short essays. You may copy and distribute these pages.

An Answer Key is provided at the back of the book for each Test. Answers to essay questions are, of necessity, incomplete and only suggestive. Students' answers should be more fully developed.

Writer's Forum

Suggestions for writing are presented under the **Writer's Forum** heading throughout this guide. You may choose from these suggestions or substitute your own creative-writing ideas.

Each Writer's Forum includes both instruction and directions for a particular writing task. Students will write in a variety of genres relating to the text and their own experience of the text. As you plan lessons, allow enough time for students to engage in the writing process:

- **Prewrite** (brainstorm and plan their work)
- **Draft** (give a shape to their ideas on paper)
- **Review** (revisit their work with an eye to improving it, on their own as well as with peers, with you, or with others)
- **Revise** (make changes that they feel will improve their draft)
- **Proofread** (check for accuracy in grammar, mechanics, and spelling)
- **Publish** (present their work to others in some way)

Notes to the Teacher

INTRODUCING THE LITERATURE

Students will be better prepared to become involved with the work of literature if they can place it in a context. The process of **contextualizing** a work of literature begins with **prior knowledge** about the book, the author, the genre, and the subject. A class discussion is a good forum for this to take place. After you have found out what, if any, familiarity students have with the book and author, and what they have been able to discern about the genre and subject, you can provide any necessary background know-ledge and, if it seems appropriate, correct any misapprehensions students have. See **Strategy 1: Beginning a Book,** pages 10–11.

Explain that in a work of fiction, an author creates an imaginary world. An important task in beginning a literature selection is to come to terms with that world. Point out that it is possible to consciously assess one's own understanding of literature and that this process is called **metacognitive reflection.** You may wish to model this process using a **think-aloud** approach as you go through the material on pages 10–11. To do this, simply read aloud the portions of *The Giver* needed to answer the questions, and speak aloud your thoughts as you formulate your responses, making explicit the connections and prior knowledge you are using in developing your thoughts.

After students have a beginning notion of the context of a work, you can proceed with the prereading activities that students will use prior to every chapter.

Sample Lesson Plan

Engaging **Prereading** activities include the following.

- Preview vocabulary and do a vocabulary exercise.
- Review the events of the previous chapter.
- Based on what they already know, have students examine their expectations about what will happen next, but be ready for surprises. Have students consider the chapter title and any illustrations. If you wish, you can use a prediction guide. Students can fill in the guide as a class, in groups, or individually.

During Reading students read with their Reader Response Journals. (You may wish to give them some of the journal and discussion topics before or after they read a particular portion of text.)

Remind students of the questions that can help them to begin to understand a work of literature (see page 11). You may wish to have students address these questions in their journals as they begin the book. Encourage students to continue using this kind of self-questioning in their Reader Response Journals.

Additional journal activities students can use with every chapter include the following.

- A summary of the events of the chapter
- Evaluations of the characters and/or text
- Questions about what they have read
- Associations they have made between the text and other texts, experiences, or situations
- Notes on the images the text evoked
- Notes on the feelings the texts evoked

After Reading, students complete the Journal and Discussion Topics, the Writer's Forum and Strategy Pages, if any, and the Test.

Bibliography

As you and your students immerse yourselves in this work of literature, you may wish to consult other works by the same author, thematically related works, video and/or audio productions of the work, and criticism. Here is a brief list of works that may be useful:

Adams, Richard. *Watership Down*.

Berry, James. *Ajeemah and His Son*.

Bishop, Claire Huchet. *Twenty and Ten*.

Frank, Anne. *Diary of a Young Girl*.

Golding, William. *Lord of the Flies*.

Hinton, SE. *The Outsiders*.

Jacques, Brian. *Redwall*.

L'Engle, Madeleine. *A Wrinkle in Time; A Swiftly Tilting Planet; The Wind in the Door*.

Lowry, Lois. *Number the Stars*.

Orwell, George. *1984*.

Pullman, Philip. *The Golden Compass*.

Vonnegut, Kurt. *Harrison Bergeron*.

White, T.H. *The Sword in the Stone*.

Strategy 1 Beginning a Book

*Directions:
Read the explanation, then complete the exercises.*

When an artist or craftworker sets about creating a work, there are a set of standard tools, techniques, and products available for him or her to choose from. The choreographer, for example, can choose from a wide variety of styles of dance: folk/ethnic, ballet, modern, jazz, tap, break, hip hop, disco, contact improvisation, etc. An infinite variety of steps, gestures, and movements may be combined and then complemented with make-up, masks, costumes, stage settings, and music in order to create an impression, set a mood, make a statement, or tell a story. The choreographer may borrow from sports like gymnastics or languages that rely on movement, like American Sign Language, or create elements that come from everyday life or are completely new. The product may be a solo, a pas de deux (duet), a line dance, etc. And the techniques used may include certain conventions, such as theme and variations and repetition, which the choreographer may choose to employ or not. The choreographer cannot and does not use every technique and style in each dance, and each choreographer's choices are guided by his or her goal, which might be the answer to a question such as, "How can I effectively communicate my vision?" The viewer coming to see the finished dance sees it over time, and may not be able to take in the whole at once. There is usually no opportunity for a second look. Attending to detail, shape, movement, rhythm, pattern, and the effect of the whole, the viewer brings his or her past experience to bear and can come to understand the dance in some meaningful way.

The writer is an artist who works in words that create images, thoughts, and feelings in the reader. Like the choreographer, the writer works to communicate a vision to people without speaking to them directly in conversation. The reader's understanding of the standard tools, techniques, products, and conventions of the writer helps the reader to comprehend the writer's vision. But at the same time that we try to understand the writer's communication, we must acknowledge that each reader also brings an individual and unique understanding to the act of reading, and so no two readers will experience a book in exactly the same way, just as no two viewers will have identical experiences of a dance. Different readers will have different insights and feelings, so discussion between and among readers can enrich the experience of all.

Beginning a book is particularly important, because readers starting a book are entering a new and uncharted territory. When you are starting a book, paying particular attention to the writer's use of tools, techniques, and conventions can help.

TITLE: It is a convention for a novel to have a title, found on the front cover, the spine, and the title page. The title of the book may explicitly tell what the book is about, may hint about the story, or may seem very mysterious. Depending on the title, you may feel interested, curious, hopeful, etc. The author's name follows immediately after the title. If you know anything about the author already, for example, that Lowry has written about the Holocaust, it might help you make predictions about the content of the book.

BOOK JACKET: Most books have a picture on the cover. The writer may or may not have had a voice in what appears, so the illustration may not represent the writer's vision. In this case, Lowry took the jacket photos herself. You will find the credit on the front inside flap.

COVER: The cover under the jacket may also have an illustration, or it may be fairly plain. Note the color, design, and texture. As you read, consider whether it has some meaning in relation to the text.

COPYRIGHT PAGE: The copyright page tells the dates of the book's publication. It can help you know whether the book is recent or older.

OTHER BOOKS BY: Sometimes there is a list that names other books by the same author. If you are familiar with any of these other works, you may have some idea of what is to come. This is also true if you have heard about the book from friends, read a book review, heard the book on audiotape, or seen a movie version. This is some of your prior knowledge about the book.

TABLE OF CONTENTS: While some books have unnamed divisions, sometimes authors title their chapters. Lowry has chosen to use untitled divisions.

INSIDE ILLUSTRATIONS: Some books are illustrated throughout with drawings, paintings, photographs, etc. This book is not.

BOOK JACKET BLURBS: The notes on the back and inside front flap are advertising, meant to give away enough of the story to pique your interest and convince you to buy the book. The back blurb for *The Giver* is a quotation from page 64 of the book. But the inside front flap has analysis, which (in my opinion) you should skip because it gives away part of the plot and will interfere with your reading of the book.

FIRST FEW PARAGRAPHS: The first few paragraphs of the story provide the writer with the opportunity to introduce the characters, plot, setting, and theme of the story. Read carefully to learn as much as you can about the world of the book.

1. What is your reaction to the title of the book?
2. Based on the title, what do you think this book will be about?
3. Describe the jacket illustration. What can you gather from it?
4. How long has it been since this book was first published?
5. What, if anything, do you already know about Lowry, her works, or *The Giver*?
6. What literary award has this book won? What does that signify to you?

Read to the space on page 4 and answer the following questions:

7. What is the narrator like? Can you trust the narrator's perceptions? How did you decide?
8. Who seem(s) to be the most important character(s)? How can you tell?
9. Where does the story take place? Is it a real setting or one created by the author? What special characteristics does the setting have?
10. What clues are there to the genre of this story?
11. What does the focus of the story seem to be?
12. What do you predict will happen next in the story?
13. What more do you want to know about the setting and the characters?

Chapter 1

Journal and Discussion Topics

1. Now that you've read the first chapter, what do you think the story will be about? What evidence supports your conclusion? Have your ideas changed significantly? Explain.
2. Pay attention to first impressions, and to changes in your impressions of characters and the community, as you read and note them.
3. What unexpected or unusual uses of language do you notice in this chapter? What do you think is the purpose of each?
4. What is the community like?
5. What does Jonas's attention to careful, accurate language mean to you?
6. How would you feel if your family had a feelings ritual like the one in which Jonas's family participates?
7. What do you think happens when someone is released?

Vocabulary

intrigued: 1, very interested; fascinated
rasping: 2, grating; rough sounding
upturned: 2, turned toward the sky
churn: 2, move uncomfortably
navigational: 2, having to do with steering
ironic: 2, contrast between tone/meaning
jeering: 3, mocking
palpable: 3, able to be felt
patriotic: 3, inspired by love of country
hymn: 3, song of praise
hatchery: 4, place for hatching fish eggs
distraught: 4, mentally upset

tunic: 4, long outer garment
apprehensive: 4, fearful about the future
wheedle: 5, beg with soft words
defiant: 5, resisting or challenging
nurturer: 7, one who helps another grow
supplementary: 7, additional
capacity: 8, ability
adequately: 8, sufficiently; completely
transgression: 9, breaking of a law or rule
soothed: 9, calmed
awed: 9, struck with wonder
beckoning: 10, motioning someone to come closer

Summary

As December approaches, Jonas is trying to accurately identify the emotion he feels. It is not fright, which he had felt the previous year when an unidentified aircraft flew over his community, although aircraft are forbidden to pass over. The appearance of the unidentified plane caused general consternation, and people stopped to wait for an explanation. Instead, they received orders from a voice over a loudspeaker to go inside immediately. Unquestioningly, they all immediately took shelter. A few minutes later, the explanation came: a Pilot-in-Training had made a mistake, and as a result, would be "released" as a punishment. Jonas recalls once having taunted the ineptness of his friend Asher, saying "You're released," and being seriously chastised.

In contrast to Jonas, who is careful about language, Asher is a master of the malapropism and the not-quite-right word. Jonas recalls one time when Asher said "distraught" when "distracted" was more appropriate. Recalling this, as he puts away his bicycle, Jonas decides that *apprehensive* is the proper word to describe his feelings as he waits for what December will bring his group, the Elevens.

A white space on the page marks the passage of time. After dinner that night, Jonas's family has a ritual of sharing feelings. Jonas's sister, Lily, a Seven, tells about becoming angry on the playground when a rule was not followed. Father, a Nurturer responsible for the care of newchildren until they are placed with families, tells about one of the newchildren who is not growing well and may have to be released. Release for newchildren and elderly persons is not a punishment, as it is for transgressors like the errant pilot, who violate community rules. For newchildren it is sad, and for the elderly it is a celebration of their full life. Father suggests asking if he can bring this particular newchild home for extra nurturing—a very unusual measure—and the rest of the family agrees. Mother, who works in the Justice Department, tells of her frustration in dealing with a repeat offender who has committed a second transgression. She thought he had reformed, and she knows that if he commits a third offense, he will automatically be released. Jonas shares his apprehension about the upcoming Ceremony of Twelve in December. Mother sends Lily to get ready for bed so that she and Father can have a private discussion with Jonas.

Strategy 2

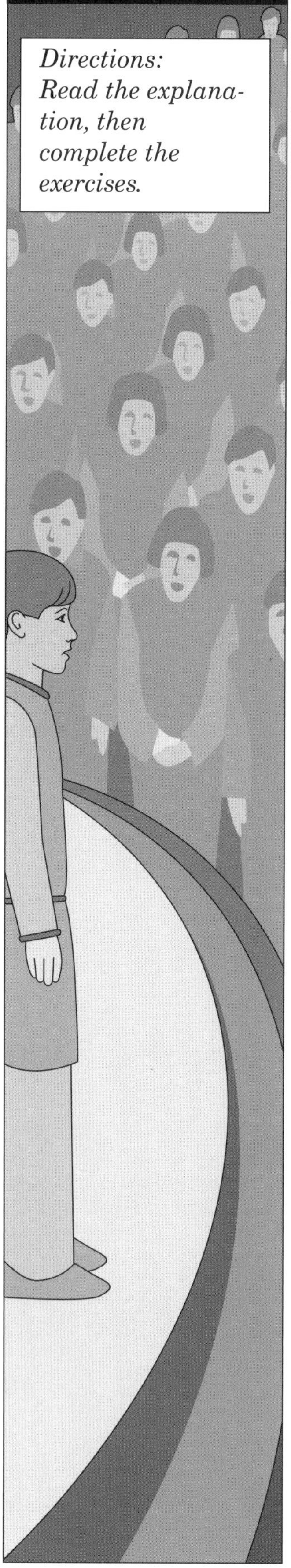

Setting and Mood

Directions:
Read the explanation, then complete the exercises.

Setting is both the world in which the story takes place and the changing scenery that serves as the backdrop for each scene or chapter. Setting includes what the characters see, hear, smell, and can touch in their environment. Sights include

- Time of day
- Season of the year
- Plants and animals
- Natural features
- Weather
- Landscape
- Buildings or other structures

The general setting of this story is the community, a place with no animals and a lot of strictly enforced rules and customs. The particular setting within the community changes from scene to scene and chapter to chapter.

Settings can serve different functions in different stories, and at different times in the same story. It may be a mere backdrop to the story, or it may have a more integral part. The setting may be symbolic and a source of information about the inhabitants of the area. The setting may create conflicts for the characters of the story. The setting may help or hinder the characters in achieving their goal. It may provide materials or resources that help the characters solve problems, or create physical hardships or challenges that are difficult to overcome. Setting also helps establish characterization (see Strategy 6). Notice how little physical description of setting occurs in the first chapters of this book. The setting of a story affects how we and the characters feel about their surroundings. This feeling is called **Mood.** The setting can make things seem pleasant, or create an air of foreboding that hints to readers that something bad is about to happen.

Although a novel like *The Giver* is classified as a narrative—that is, a type of writing that tells a story—sections of a novel that deal with the setting are usually passages of description. Look for these later in the book.

As you notice the setting, try to figure out what the writer is trying to convey. Pay attention to the possibilities and problems created by the setting, and the mood the setting creates for you, in order to take advantage of hints the writer is giving about what might happen next.

Extend the following chart to create a record of *The Giver* settings and their functions.

Page #	Setting Description	Function(s) in Story

Strategy 3

Irony

Directions: Read the explanation, then complete the exercises.

Irony is a term from a Greek word meaning "someone who hides under a false appearance." When irony is used, things appear to be different, even the opposite, of what they really are: unexpected events happen, what people say is not what they mean. Authors use irony to create interest, surprise, or an understanding with their readers that the characters do not share. There are three types of irony.

Verbal irony is irony in the use of language. Verbal irony means that what is said is different from or the opposite of what is meant. A difference between tone of voice and the content of what is said is one kind of verbal irony. When the voice on the loudspeaker tells the grim fact that the Pilot-in-Training will be "released" in a voice touched with amusement, the startling difference between the content and the tone makes the statement ironic.

Understatement is another type of verbal irony. When the narrator says of the plane incident, "But it had been nothing," on page 2, and then we learn that the pilot is going to suffer a terrible punishment, the statement is revealed to be a dramatic understatement, and very ironic.

In **dramatic irony,** there is knowledge that the narrator makes available to the reader, but the characters are unaware of. In this story, Lowry uses foreshadowing (see Strategy 5)—hints in the text that suggest things to the readers without saying them directly—as one means of creating dramatic irony.

Situational irony can occur either from the point of view of a character or that of the reader. It describes a situation in which something that is expected with a great deal of certainty doesn't happen (this can be from either point of view) or in which something that is intended fails to materialize (this is only possible from a character's point of view, except in Choose-Your-Own Adventures or other books in which the reader participates by making a choice). When Jonas and the other members of his community are filled with fear at the sighting of the plane and expect terrible consequences, there is situational irony when it turns out (according to the voice) to have merely been a mistake.

1. Keep a record of other examples of irony in this story as you continue to read.

Writer's Forum 1 Shades of Meaning

Synonyms are sometimes defined as words that mean the same thing. This is not quite true. No two words mean exactly the same thing. Even if the denotation—the dictionary definition—is the same for two words, the connotation—the emotional associations and "flavor" the two words have—is always different. **Shades of meaning** refers to the differences found in words that are synonyms.

Some things that affect how we view a word are

- familiarity or lack of familiarity
- sound
- length
- famous occurrences
- formality/informality
- context
- emotional overtones

For example, consider the words *distraught* and *distracted*. Asher chooses an unfamiliar, important sounding, formal word that denotes extreme emotional discomfort. The Instructor suggests a more familiar, plain-sounding, informal word that denotes a temporary lapse of focus.

Jonas distinguishes between being *frightened* and being *eager* and being *apprehensive*. All three words have to do with expectation, but the sort of thing expected is different in each case. Because Lowry draws our attention to this issue, we can expect the language she uses to be precise, and we can expect that if we pay attention to her word choices, our analysis will help us reach a deeper understanding of the story.

With this in mind, consider the word *release*. To most people this word has a connotation of freedom (for example, from captivity) and positive emotional tones. Lowry has chosen to introduce it as a term to describe what the narrator calls a "terrible punishment, an overwhelming statement of failure" (page 2). This may contrast with our previous experience of the word, and make us pause and think about the language in the book. Because Lowry uses the word in this way, we need to think about whether the shades of meaning we generally attach to it are appropriate in this context.

1. Choose two paragraphs in Chapter 1 (at least 15 lines of the story), and rewrite them, changing the words to give different shades of meaning to the passage. Write a brief analysis explaining how your passage differs from Lowry's original.

Chapter 2

Journal and Discussion Topics

1. There are two instances of rule breaking in this chapter. Consider each one. Do you feel that the punishment was justified? Explain your reasoning.
2. In your family or community, how is a child's coming into a family different than the way it is described in Chapter 2?
3. Do you think it is true that Jonas and Asher will always be friends? What evidence is there in the book to support this statement? What evidence is there that Jonas may experience situational irony?
4. What kind of job do you think Jonas will get? Explain your reasoning.
5. If some older people in your community were to observe you, what job do you think they'd give you and why?
6. What is the role of The Receiver?
7. Why does the narrator refer to the elephant as an "imaginary creature" (page 19)?
8. Do you like the idea of the Ceremonies for each year? Why or why not?

Vocabulary

enhance: 12, improve by adding to
aptitude: 15, ability
appeal: 17, request that a decision be reconsidered
recreation: 18, exercise and enjoyment to balance work

Summary

Jonas and his parents recall past Ceremonies. The first one celebrated each year is the Ceremony of One at which all children born that year—always fifty in number—celebrate their first birthday, are given names, and are placed in a family. In recalling Lily's Ceremony of One, Father mentions that as a Nurturer he could have sneaked a look to find out the name of the child he would get, but he didn't. He admits, however, that he looked at the name of the newchild that will be coming to their house so that he could call him by name, in the hope that this would "enhance" the nurturing process. The child's name is to be Gabriel, but Father calls him Gabe for short.

Father then recalls being an Eleven himself and waiting for the Ceremony of Twelve that comes at the end of the second day of the Ceremonies. He mentions in passing that his sister turned Nine that year and received her bicycle, and that he, like almost all other older siblings, had already taught his sister to ride, although technically he was breaking a rule by doing so. He explains to Jonas that there was very little suspense for him though, because he had always been drawn to working with the newchildren, and with such an obvious aptitude, he was fairly certain of what his Assignment would be. But Jonas is not.

Mother points out that after the Ceremony of Twelve, Jonas will no longer have volunteer hours and recreation hours, and so he will no longer be spending time exclusively with his groupmates—his Assignment will take priority. Jonas insists that he and Asher, at least, will always be friends. Lily interrupts, pointing out that she is waiting for her "comfort object"—an elephant, which is referred to as an "imaginary creature." Father takes Lily to bed, Mother opens her briefcase to do some work, and Jonas does his schoolwork, still wondering about his Assignment.

Writer's Forum 2   Anecdote

An **anecdote** is a short, self-contained, interesting or humorous story. Like any other narrative, an anecdote has a plot with a beginning, middle, and end. It also generally has characters, sometimes even a main character. But unlike most narratives, it often does not have a well-developed setting, and very little, if any, character development. Also, unlike other types of narratives, it is likely to have a moral or a punchline, or some other fairly explicit way of stating what the point is. And there usually isn't much room for interpretation of that point.

Anecdotes are used frequently in conversation. In writing, they are often used in dialogue or in flashbacks (see Strategy 5).

The brief recollection about Andrei is an anecdote. It makes the point that the Elders, through their careful observations and selections, are able to make suitable assignments. The story about Asher's apology in Chapter 1 is another anecdote. It bears on the subject of careful word choice that is on Jonas's mind.

1. Write an anecdote explaining one of the items below. You may make up details as long as they are consistent with the story so far.
   a. how the community got started
   b. why the community has not got a name
   c. how people came to believe that elephants are not real creatures
   d. why The Receiver bears that name
   e. how the needle-nosed plane really came to be over the community

Chapter 3

Journal and Discussion Topics

1. What do you think of the way differences are treated in the community?
2. Why do you think Lowry focuses four paragraphs on the subject of pale eyes at the beginning of the chapter and then refers to this physical feature again at the end of the chapter?
3. What do you think of the way Lowry has chosen to convey the voice of the Speakers?
4. What do you think happened with the apple?

Vocabulary

chastise: 20, punish
unsettling: 20, upsetting
chastisement: 20, punishment
rarity: 21, unusual occurrence
petulantly: 22, with temporary ill humor
acknowledged: 22, accepted
reluctantly: 22, without real desire
droning: 22, going on and on monotonously
dangling: 23, hanging down
hoarded: 23, saved secretly

remorse: 23, sorrow for doing something wrong
disposed: 23, got rid of
bewildered: 23, confused
bewilderment: 23, confusion
nondescript: 24, with no outstanding features
mystified: 24, puzzled
conviction: 25, certainty
reflective: 25, thoughtful
renewal: 25, refreshment; recovery
solemn: 25, serious

Summary

Father brings the newchild Gabriel home, and Lily immediately notices and points out Gabriel's light-colored eyes—a rarity in the community that Jonas shares. Jonas is upset that Lily has pointed out this difference. But he thinks that light eyes have depth and give intimations of things hidden and as yet undiscovered. While Lily and Mother discuss how little honor there is in being a Birthmother, Jonas goes to his desk to do his homework.

Lily, seeing that Gabriel is sleeping, says that she'd better be quiet; and Jonas's reflection that she is never quiet, leads him to imagine her as a Speaker. He then recalls a time when the Speaker made an announcement about him, reminding male Elevens not to take food from the recreation area, and he reviews the incident that led to his breaking the rule. He had been playing catch with Asher with an apple, when something about the appearance of the apple changed—something he had no words to describe. Asher had seen nothing. Jonas had taken the apple to try to investigate further, but was not able to discover anything. Then the Speaker had announced his transgression to everybody. He tries to put the incident aside and study before dinner, while the rest of his family attends to Gabriel, who has begun to whimper. The last line of the chapter recalls Gabriel's pale eyes to the reader's attention.

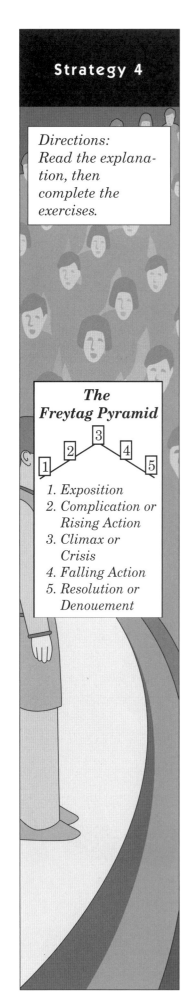

Directions: Read the explanation, then complete the exercises.

The Freytag Pyramid

1. Exposition
2. Complication or Rising Action
3. Climax or Crisis
4. Falling Action
5. Resolution or Denouement

Strategy 4 Plot—The Design of a Story

There are exciting stories and dull stories. There are westerns, adventure stories, mysteries, romances, thrillers, horror stories, science fiction stories, and fantasies. There are stories with happy endings and stories with sad endings. These differences can make stories seem worlds apart. But almost all stories—whether they are long or short, for adults or young people—have common characteristics that make them stories.

Every story has a **plot** or sequence of actions, a setting or settings where the action takes place, a character or group of characters who take action, and a narrator who tells the story to the reader.

People who study literature have come up with several different ways of talking about plot. When people talk about stories with young children, they often refer to the beginning, the middle, and the end. This is not just a notion for little kids. These 3 parts are the way screenwriters and television writers arrange their scripts. Dramatists, on the other hand, often work with a 5-act play. The 5 acts each represents an essential and sequential part of the drama. Narrative is also often presented in high school and college classes as having a 5-part structure as follows:

1. **Exposition:** introduction of essential background information, as well as characters, situations, and conflicts. Exposition may be found throughout a story, as well as at the beginning.
2. **Complication or Rising Action:** the beginning of the central conflict in the story.
3. **Crisis:** (sometimes called the **turning point**) usually the point at which the main character's action or choice determines the outcome of the conflict or climax.
4. **Falling Action:** the time when all the pieces fall into place and make the ending inevitable.
5. **Resolution or Denouement:** when the conflicts are resolved and the story is concluded.

So do we look at a story as having 5 parts or 3 parts? One way we can think about this is to see where the 5 parts fit into the beginning, middle, and end:

BEGINNING: Exposition

MIDDLE: Complication, ends with the Crisis

END: Climax (the beginning of the end) and Resolution

Writers adapt the plot structure to a particular story. They decide how much exposition should be included and where, how many conflicts there are, and what's told to the reader, and what is left for the reader to figure out.

1. As you read *The Giver,* pause at the end of each chapter, and identify for yourself where it fits in the plot structure. Place it on a Freytag Pyramid of your own. Note the places in the story that you find the beginning of each of the five parts. The shape of your pyramid may not exactly match the model in the margin.

Chapter 4

Journal and Discussion Topics

1. In what areas of life do the members of the community have free choice, and in what areas are their lives regulated?
2. Do you think the rule against bragging is a good one? Why or why not?
3. Read the second full paragraph on page 27 beginning, "The area of dwellings behind him. . . ." What kind of description of the setting is included? What is NOT included?
4. What advantages and disadvantages does Jonas see in the way he decided to distribute his volunteer hours?
5. What similarities are there between the newchildren and the Old?
6. When Larissa says that Roberto raised "two very successful children," what do you think she means by *successful?*
7. What do you think about release now?

Vocabulary

regulated: 26, controlled
invariably: 26, without change
gravitating: 26, moving toward
rehabilitation: 26, recovery from an injury
bypass: 27, sleep
tabulated: 28, counted up; kept track of
disgrace: 28, loss of honor; embarrassment
serene: 28, calm and peaceful

distribution: 29, sending from a central location
frail: 30, physically weak
exposed: 30, not covered
absorbent: 31, capable of soaking up moisture
confided: 31, told with trust
chortled: 33, chuckled
hooted: 33, laughed loudly

Summary

Almost at the end of his volunteer hours, Jonas goes looking for Asher so they can work together. As he searches, he thinks about the freedom of choice allowed in deciding where to spend volunteer hours—a freedom that is rare in the community. He thinks about Benjamin who accomplished an enormous amount by focusing his volunteer hours at the Rehabilitation Center, but reflects that he could never speak to Benjamin about these accomplishments because of the rule against bragging. He finds Asher at the House of the Old with another Eleven, Fiona. They are in the bathing room, helping to wash the Old.

Jonas thinks to himself that he is glad he has spread his volunteer hours around, because he has been able to see the differences in the various functions of the community. But, he reflects, this has left him with no idea of what his Assignment might be. As Jonas bathes Larissa, he reflects on the similarity between bathing her and bathing Gabriel, and on the fact that the old and the young are the only ones whose bodies can be seen naked without apology. Larissa describes the wonderful release of Roberto that occurred that morning. She contrasts this with the boring release of Edna shortly before. Jonas asks about the ceremony, and Larissa describes the telling of Roberto's life, the toast, the anthem, Roberto's speech, and people's answering speeches. Jonas probes further, asking what release actually entails. Larissa can only tell him that Roberto walked through a special door with a look of pure happiness, and was gone. Jonas wishes he had been present, but children aren't allowed to attend release ceremonies.

Chapter 5

Journal and Discussion Topics

1. What do you think of the dream-telling ritual?
2. At one point, the clean up of meals is referred to in this chapter. How do you think meals are prepared and served? Explain why you think as you do.
3. Explain in your own words what happened to Jonas in this chapter and what effect the pills have on him.
4. Why do you think "Stirrings" are treated with pills in this community?

Vocabulary

disquieting: 34, upsetting
infraction: 34, violation
good-naturedly: 38, with characteristic good humor

Summary

At the family ritual of dream telling, Jonas (who usually does not dream) has a dream to share, although it is difficult for him to tell because he feels a little embarrassed. The dream began in the bathing room of the House of the Old, but it was different from the real room in having only one tub, not rows of them. Only Jonas and Fiona were there, and he was trying to convince her to get into the tub and let him bathe her, although he knew that she wouldn't and that she shouldn't.

Father asks Lily to walk along with him as he goes to work, leaving Mother and Jonas alone. Mother explains that the feeling of wanting that Jonas experienced was what is called "first Stirrings," something that happens to everyone and often begins with a dream. Jonas has heard from the Speaker that Stirrings must be reported and treated, and he is concerned that this will be a complicated process and interfere with his life. He is relieved to discover that it only means that he must take a pill every morning. His mother gives him one, and within minutes, before he even reaches school, the feelings of the Stirrings are gone.

Strategy 5

Foreshadowing and Flashback

Directions: Read the explanation, then complete the exercises.

Writers do not always tell plot events in chronological order. For one thing, they may hint at events before they occur. This is called **foreshadowing,** and it lets readers know beforehand something about what is going to happen later. This technique helps create suspense and irony and keeps the reader involved in the unfolding plot.

Foreshadowing may come from a character, from the setting, or from the narrator. For example, Jonas's experience of the change in the apple, which is contrasted with Asher's inability to perceive the change, is a foreshadowing that Jonas, despite all the emphasis on Sameness, is different. This suggests that sooner or later he will come into conflict with a community that promotes Sameness.

Writers may also go back to material that happened prior to the beginning of the story or earlier in the plot sequence. This is called **flashback.** Flashbacks give the reader background material that is necessary for understanding the story. Sometimes they take the form of anecdotes. Flashbacks may come from the narrator or the characters. When Jonas is in the House of the Old and recalls Gabriel's bath the previous night, this is an example of a flashback.

1. Find another example of a flashback. What essential information does it contain?

2. As you continue reading, find as many examples as you can of foreshadowing. Are they from characters, the setting, or the narrator? Did you realize they were foreshadowings when you read them, or only later?

Writer's Forum 3   A List of Rules

Rules are a set of guidelines that people agree to share or are forced to follow. Sets of rules usually include an explanation of the consequences for failure to observe the rules, and list exemptions and exceptions.

Rules often begin with words like the following:

- Do
- Always
- Every
- If

- Don't
- Never
- Whenever
- No

Rules only work if they are clear, workable, and accepted by the community they were made for. It is usually best to keep rules short, and have the minimum number possible.

With a group of classmates, make a set of rules for a community to which you belong or for a particular activity you do together. Tell why each rule is important for the community.

Name _____

Vocabulary

Look at each group of words. Tell why it is important in the story.

1. hoarded, remorse, disposed _____

   _____

2. gravitating, tabulated, rehabilitation _____

   _____

3. bewildered, bewilderment, nondescript, mystified _____

   _____

4. chortled, hooted, frail_____

   _____

Essay Topics

1. Look back at the predictions you made about the book for Strategy 1. Write your opinion of your earlier predictions based on what you know now. Make new predictions for the rest of the book.

2. This story has what might be called a futuristic setting. Think of another story you know that has a futuristic setting. Tell what is similar and what is different about the two settings.

3. *The Giver* could be described as a coming-of-age story. Jonas is waiting to find out what his role in the community will be. Think of another story in which a young person chooses or is given a job or a role as he or she becomes an adult member of his or her community. Discuss the similarities and the differences between the plot in the story you've chosen and that of *The Giver* so far.

4. What's your favorite moment in the story so far? Explain your choice.

5. Which character is your favorite? Tell why.

6. Roberto seems to be healthy and lively and in possession of all his faculties. Why should someone like Roberto be released, whatever it means?

7. What good elements do you find in the society of the community? What seems inappropriate to you? Explain your reasons.

8. Why do you think Eights usually choose to do their first volunteer hours on Recreation Duty?

Chapter 6

Journal and Discussion Topics

1. What do you think of the pledge the family has to sign about Gabriel?
2. Why, according to the narrator, would it have been especially sad if they had needed to release Gabriel? What do you think of this?
3. What do you think of the concept of a replacement child?
4. What, if anything, strikes you as strange about the Ceremony of Loss?
5. Does the community distinction between release and Loss make sense to you? Explain.
6. What do you think of the description of the impact Fritz's transgressions have on the community?
7. Draw a picture of one of the Ceremonies.
8. Do you think it would be possible in our world to have a match-making service with a 100% success rate, like the one in the community? Why or why not?
9. Do you have the same certainty as Jonas that his Assignment will be the right one? Why or why not?
10. What signs of independence have you had in your life?

Vocabulary

designated: 40, showed
interdependence: 40, depending on each other
emblem: 41, symbol
stowed: 41, put away
throng: 41, crowd
indulgently: 42, with forgiveness
reprieve: 42, release from consequences
on behalf: 42, in support of
inadequate: 42, not meeting expectations
relinquish: 42, give up or give back
exuberant: 44, joyful
somber: 44, serious, melancholy
consciousness: 44, awareness
dutifully: 45, fulfill expectations
cringed: 45, shrank back in fear

podium: 45, a platform for a public speaker
infringed: 46, trespassed on
distinguishing: 46, identifying
discarded: 46, thrown out
unaccustomed: 47, unusual
sanitation: 47, pertaining to removal of trash
boyishness: 47, energy and humor of a boy
buoyancy: 48, ability to float
meticulously: 48, particular attention to detail
disposition: 48, mood or attitude
correspond: 48, match
interact: 48, to act on each other
monitored: 48, checked on
scrupulously: 49, with great care

Summary

At the Ceremonies, Jonas and Lily sit with their groupmates, Father with the Nurturers until the Ceremony of One is over, and Mother with other parents. Gabriel is not at the Ceremony, but through Father's intervention he has received a reprieve and is allowed to have an additional year of nurturing before Naming and Placement, rather than being released. At the Naming ceremony, there is a special Placement in which a child who had accidentally drowned is replaced by another child of the same name. As the lost child had been honored with the Ceremony of Loss, the new child is honored with the Murmur-of-Replacement Ceremony.

The last day of ceremonies begins with the Ceremony of Nine, at which children receive their bicycles, followed by the Tens, who receive adult haircuts. Female Elevens receive new undergarments and males get longer trousers with a calculator pocket. At lunch, the Elevens discuss rumors of people who left the community because they weren't happy with their Assignment. Asher's mother told him that about ten years previously someone had really applied for Elsewhere and been released, without even a ceremony. Jonas shrugs it off. He believes that the meticulous planning that invariably creates successful spouse matching and newchild placements will lead to appropriate Assignments.

Strategy 6   Characterization

Directions: Read the explanation, then complete the exercises.

A **Character** in a story is someone or something whose actions, choices, thoughts, ideas, words, and influence are important in developing the plot. Characters are often people, but also include other living creatures, and sometimes even non-living things. A force, such as good or evil, can operate as a character in a story.

Most stories have a single character or a small group of characters whose goal or problem is the core of the plot. This character or group of characters is called the **protagonist.** The protagonist does not have to be good, but a good protagonist may be referred to as the "hero" of the story. Readers usually identify with the protagonist and hope that the protagonist will succeed in attaining his or her goal. The character, group, or force that opposes the protagonist is called the **antagonist.** In certain stories, this character may be referred to as the villain (see Strategy 8).

Characters, whether human or not, have what we call "personality"—a set of characteristic traits and features by which we recognize them. Personality is what helps us distinguish one community member from another community member, one Eleven from another Eleven.

Characterization is the name for the techniques a writer uses to reveal the personality of characters to the reader. Characterization is achieved in a number of different ways:

- **Words:** comments by the narrator, dialogue by others about the character, as well as the character's own words; what is said, as well as *how* it is said—dialect, slang, tone—are important
- **Thoughts:** what's going on in the character's mind, the character's motives and choices
- **Appearance:** the character's physical characteristics and clothing
- **Actions:** what the character does
- **Interactions:** how the character relates to others
- **Names:** often symbolic of a major character trait or role
- **Chosen Setting:** the items, furnishings, etc., that the character chooses to surround him- or herself with
- **Change/Development:** the occurrence of and direction of change or development that a character undergoes inwardly

1. What techniques does Lowry NOT use for characterization?

2. What is the effect on you of only the children and the Old being named?

3. How does Asher interact with others?

4. What changes in Jonas's character have you seen so far in the story?

5. How would you characterize Father and his role in the story so far?

Chapter 7

Journal and Discussion Topics

1. How would you characterize the Chief Elder?
2. What do you think of the ritual of thanking people—for example, for their feelings, their dreams, and their childhood?
3. Do the Assignments given out seem appropriate to you? Explain.
4. Why do you think the Chief Elder skips Jonas? Give as many possibilities as you can.

Vocabulary

impulse: 52, sudden desire or wish
devised: 52, invented
nourishment: 52, food
pampered: 53, taken special care of
impose: 53, force
prestige: 53, honor; esteem; respect
acquisition: 54, learning
retroactive: 54, applying to a prior period

wielded: 54, used
precision: 55, exactness
lapse: 55, failure to meet a standard
escalating: 55, growing greater; increasing
studious: 56, naturally inclined to study
dazed: 57, stunned
avert: 57, turn aside

Summary

For the Ceremony of Twelve, Elevens sit in birth order and are again referred to by the number of birth order, as they were before the Naming ceremony. Jonas is Nineteen, and is seated between Fiona (Eighteen) and Pierre (Twenty). The Chief Elder gives an opening speech in which she discusses the importance of Assignment and the talents of the group before her. She points out that the years of childhood are spent learning Sameness, but in the Ceremony of Twelve, differences are honored by Assignments that are created to fit individual inclinations and abilities.

Now the Chief Elder begins the Assignments, reviewing each Eleven's qualifications and life history and explaining how the choice was made. One is chosen to be a Fish Hatchery Attendant. Two is assigned to be a Birthmother. Three is given the Assignment of Instructor of Sixes. Each Assignment seems just right for the skills and personality of the person chosen. The narrator dwells on the Assignment of Four, Jonas's friend Asher, as Assistant Director of Recreation, recalling Asher's trouble with precise language and his good humor. With Asher, as with each other new Twelve, the Chief Elder ends by thanking him for his childhood.

After a white space indicating the passage of time, and a summary of the intervening Assignments, we come to Fiona, who is chosen to be Caretaker of the Old. But then, instead of calling Jonas, the Chief Elder skips number Nineteen and calls Twenty, continuing on after with Twenty-one and Twenty-two. Jonas is confused, dazed, mortified, and horrified, afraid to look at his parents for support because he supposes he must have done something to shame them. But he doesn't know what he could have done wrong.

Strategy 7   Forming Hypotheses

Directions: Read the explanation, then complete the exercises.

Sometimes we make guesses about causes, results, and intentions. When we guess, we may rely on intuition or what we wish to be true more than anything else. A **hypothesis** is special in that it is an *educated* guess. Unlike a "regular" guess, it is a prediction based on evidence.

Some people associate the word *hypothesis* strictly with scientific investigation. But that is not the limit of its application. Readers are constantly making and testing hypotheses about story characters' reasons for acting and making choices, about what will happen next in the plot, and about the author's intentions. Here are some criteria for a good hypothesis:

- **It should be of significance in the world of the story.** In some stories (for example, Charles Dickens' *A Tale of Two Cities*), characters' physical appearances are extremely important. In reading that book, it makes sense to formulate hypotheses about the possible meanings and plot developments that will result from the striking similarity between the looks of two characters. In reading *The Giver,* forming hypotheses based on physical appearance generally does NOT make sense because the characters' physical qualities are barely mentioned. The one exception is the unusual occurrence of pale or light eyes, on which Lowry focuses in Chapter 3. When Lowry draws attention to this physical feature, it is a signal to the reader that light eyes are a good basis for making a hypothesis. What do they mean? Is there or will there be a connection between Gabriel and Jonas? Who else has pale eyes?

- **It should be clearly stated and specific so that you can easily tell what it means, but it should reach beyond what you know for certain.** If you formed a hypothesis: *Maybe light eyes are important in the story,* it would not do you any good. That light eyes are significant is something we have already established. A hypothesis is a statement that you do not yet know the truth of.

- **It should identify the motivation, result, or intention that you think you have identified.** For example, we know that something changed in the way that Jonas saw the apple. Given the evidence, you might form the following hypothesis: *Maybe light eyes have to do with a special way of seeing.* Once you form a hypothesis, you should look for further information to verify or disprove it.

1. Form a hypothesis about what will drive the important action of the plot of *The Giver*. What will the central conflict be?

   - Collect and record evidence that supports your hypothesis.
   - Now write your hypothesis along with the evidence that supports it. You may wish to arrange the evidence in order of decreasing importance (most important point first) or increasing importance (most important point last).
   - Finally, as you continue reading, add a paragraph to your paper after each chapter, with a revision of your hypothesis based on new information and insights.

Chapter 8

Journal and Discussion Topics

1. What is unusual about The Receiver? What meaning do you find in this?
2. How is it possible that Jonas never noticed The Receiver before?
3. Ten years before, the Committee of Elders failed in their selection of a Receiver. What else happened ten years before? Tell if you think the two events might be connected and how.
4. What makes choosing a Receiver exceptionally difficult?
5. What do you think a Receiver of Memory might do? Could anyone in our country/culture be considered a Receiver of Memory? In other countries/cultures that you know?
6. Imagine you are Jonas. What questions do you want to ask The Receiver when you meet him?

Vocabulary

piecemeal: 59, in pieces; not unified
crescendo: 59, growing louder
kinship: 59, relationship
subsided: 59, grew less
vibrant: 59, full of life and energy
gracious: 59, kind and warmly courteous
benign: 59, kind and gentle
anxiety: 59, uneasiness about the future
anguish: 60, agonizing pain
jaunty: 60, self-confident

intently: 61, with great intensity
dwell: 61, continue to focus
indolence: 61, laziness
unanimous: 62, agreement of all members
integrity: 62, honesty; moral uprightness
magnitude: 63, level
consumed: 63, destroyed
despair: 63, loss of hope
spontaneously: 64, without planning
collective: 64, made by all those present
audible: 64, able to be heard

Summary

The Chief Elder begins to speak, calming the audience's tension. She apologizes for causing anxiety to the community and anguish to Jonas, and then invites Jonas to the stage. She declares that rather than being assigned, Jonas has been selected, chosen as the next Receiver of Memory. Jonas sees the current Receiver sitting with the Committee of Elders, but separate from them, a man with pale eyes whom Jonas has never noticed before.

The Chief Elder refers to the last attempt to select a Receiver ten years previously, an attempt that failed for some undisclosed reason. The mention of this makes the audience uneasy. She explains why the process of choosing a Receiver is difficult: unlike other Assignments in which the candidate's behavior continues to be observed and addressed when necessary, the Receiver-in-Training cannot be subject to observation during training, because it occurs in private with the current Receiver. She reminds the audience that the vote of the Committee must be unanimous and without doubt, and enumerates the qualities that The Receiver must have: intelligence, integrity, courage, wisdom. Jonas, the Committee feels, has the makings of these.

But there is one other quality necessary, what the current Receiver calls the Capacity to See Beyond, which the Committee does not understand. The Chief Elder looks to Jonas to see if he will acknowledge having this ability, telling him that The Receiver says that Jonas does. At first Jonas hesitates, believing that he cannot claim this quality and that he must beg the Committee's pardon and decline the selection. But then, as he looks at the audience, he has an experience similar to what happened with the apple. He realizes that this may be the Capacity to See Beyond. The Chief Elder accepts his affirmation, and finalizes the selection. The audience murmurs his name, softly at first, then louder and louder, signaling their acceptance of his new role, and Jonas listens with a mixture of pride and fear.

Strategy 8   Evaluating a Book

Directions: Read the explanation, then complete the exercises.

In an evaluative essay, you identify the work you are considering by its title, author, and genre, briefly summarize the plot, and then state your assessment of the work.

When you write the summary, it is a good idea to include the names of the main characters, the basic plot conflict, the setting, and the background of the situation.

Your statements of judgment should include your evaluation of the work as a whole (or so far, if you have read only a portion of the work) and show how your reaction to elements of the work led you to that response. For example, you might respond positively to the following:

- the plot is suspenseful and interesting
- the themes resonate with what you believe
- you like or admire one or more of the characters
- the vivid description catches your interest
- the book is amusing and enjoyable
- you learn something valuable
- you are so absorbed that you can't wait to read more
- you find insights or understandings that enrich your life

Your evaluation does not have to include only favorable responses, however. You may judge the work unfavorably if you think, for example, that the

- dialogue is unbelievable
- characterization is weak
- characters' motivations are not believable
- plot is convoluted or unbelievable
- attitudes expressed seem inappropriate to you
- genre doesn't appeal to you

It is also possible to present a situation in which you began with one point of view, but as your reading developed, your estimation of the work changed.

1. Write an evaluation of *The Giver* so far. Use the criteria above, as well as criteria of your own, that are pertinent. As you continue reading, see if your evaluation changes.

Chapter 9

Journal and Discussion Topics

1. Jonas thinks, "Things couldn't change, with Asher" (page 66). Do you think he's right? Support your answer with evidence from the text.
2. What do you think might have happened to the female Receiver?
3. What struck you most forcibly about Jonas's rules? What struck Jonas most forcibly?
4. What could be the reasons behind Jonas's rules?
5. Do you think that other members of the community lie? Explain why you think as you do.

Vocabulary

hesitation: 65, slowness to speak or act
annex: 68, a building added onto a larger building
unrelated: 68, not connected to
intimate: 69, personal
unnerving: 69, upsetting
prohibition: 69, rule forbidding
restriction: 69, limitation
requisitioned: 69, requested from a government source
excruciating: 70, intensely painful
diminished: 70, lessened
throb: 70, pulse with pain
indescribable: 70, not capable of being described
comprehension: 70, understanding
steeled: 70, strengthened; prepared
integral: 70, essential
unintentional: 70–71, not done on purpose
utmost: 71, greatest possible
conceivably: 71, possibly

Summary

Feeling separate for the first time in his life, Jonas leaves the Auditorium and finds Asher, and they ride home together. But twice in that brief time, Jonas feels a hesitation on Asher's part when they come near the subject of Jonas's selection. At dinner, Lily is excited about beginning her volunteer hours at the Nurturing Center, while Jonas is uneasy. Father and Mother are surprised and awed by the honor paid to Jonas, but hesitant to discuss the previous selection—the one that failed. Jonas does find out from them, however, that the female who was selected is never to be mentioned by name in the community, and her name cannot ever be used again for a newchild—the most serious sign of disgrace in the community.

Jonas goes to his sleepingroom and looks over his rules, which shock him. He is dismayed that he must return home immediately after training, leaving him no time for recreation. He is startled that he is permitted to be rude, not seriously affected by the prohibition of dream-telling, and unnerved by the prohibition of medication for any pain related to training, as he recalls the Chief Elder's warning about the pain. The rule permitting him to lie shocks him, largely because it is counter to the constant drilling he has received in precision of language, which strives to omit even unintentional lies. And this rule leads him to wonder if there are others in his community who have this same rule. Allowed by his rules to ask personal questions, he imagines asking his father, "Do you lie?"—but he knows that even if he did, he would not know if the answer were true.

Strategy 9

Plot Conflict

Directions: Read the explanation, then complete the exercises.

Conflict is the core of a story's plot. Conflict is what makes us wonder if the protagonist will attain his or her goal. Conflict is what adds suspense and excitement to stories. Usually there is one overarching conflict that takes up much of the book. But each chapter or scene in the book usually also has conflict on a smaller scale.

The struggles that a protagonist undergoes in a story can be either **internal** or **external.** In an **internal** conflict, the protagonist undergoes an interior struggle. He or she might have conflicting desires, values, personality traits, and/or motives. People often have internal conflicts as they grow and develop from one stage in their lives to the next. An internal conflict takes place within the character's mind and heart.

In an **external** conflict, the protagonist struggles with something or someone outside of himself or herself. The conflict may be with another individual, with a task or problem, with society, with nature, with an idea, or with a force, such as good or evil.

In this book, as mentioned earlier, the main plot conflict is introduced late in the book. And since much of the early part of the book is taken up with giving background information, the focus is on explaining the customs of the community, not on conflict.

1. What is the overarching conflict in this story? Cite evidence to support your conclusion.

2. Make and fill in a chart like the sample below to show the main conflict for each chapter. For some chapters, you may have a difficult time identifying a conflict.

CHAPTER	CONFLICT
1	
2	
3	
4	
5	
6	
7	
8	
9	
10	
11	
12	
13	
14	
15	
16	
17	

Chapter 10

Journal and Discussion Topics

1. What do you think of the attendant's explanation of the locked door? Explain your answer.
2. What unique aspects does Jonas notice in the furnishings of The Receiver's quarters?
3. How does The Receiver treat Jonas?
4. Why are the memories that The Receiver holds important?
5. What things does Jonas learn that surprise/puzzle him?
6. Why do you think Jonas doesn't know what the words *sled, snow,* and *downhill* mean?

Vocabulary

unremarkable: 72, not special or unique
discomfort: 73, lack of peace
insure: 73, make certain of (also ensure)
relocated: 73, moved to a new place
sturdy: 74, firmly built
slender: 74, thin
alcove: 74, small area set off from a room
intricate: 74, complicated
conspicuous: 74, obvious

embossed: 74, raised from the surface
transmit: 77, transfer; give
tentatively: 77, without certainty
generations: 77, a long time
concept: 78, idea
exhilarating: 78, exciting and refreshing
accumulates: 78, builds up
runners: 78, the long blades on a sled
deftly: 79, with an easy motion

Summary

Fiona and Jonas bike together to their first day of training. Jonas has to identify himself before the door is unlocked. The Attendant stands to acknowledge Jonas's presence, and addresses him respectfully as "Receiver of Memory." She unlocks the door to The Receiver's room, and Jonas is surprised—he has never in his life encountered a locked door in the community, and now has come upon two.

In The Receiver's quarters, Jonas is aware of the uniqueness of The Receiver's furnishings. Furnishings here are beautiful, rather than merely functional, and whereas other dwellings have only three books, the Receiver's home is filled with books.

Jonas is confused when the man, whom he recognizes from the Ceremony, welcomes him as The Receiver. When Jonas interrupts him to ask a question and then apologizes, the man does not give the standard response. He explains that from the moment of Jonas's arrival, he has considered Jonas to be The Receiver. He invites Jonas to ask questions, and when Jonas is silent, he explains that he has to transmit all of the memories he has to Jonas. Jonas interrupts again, thinking that the focus is on the man's personal memories, and then apologizes. The man explains that there is no time for apologies between them, and that he is speaking of memories of the whole world, not personal memories. Jonas cannot understand the concept of generations or of anyplace other than the community. The man explains briefly, and points out that wisdom comes from the memories that are the basis for shaping the future. In trying to explain how the memories weigh him down, the man uses the metaphor of a sled, and realizing that Jonas does not understand, he decides to transmit a memory of snow and sledding. He begins by turning the speaker in the room off, another thing that Jonas has never in his life witnessed.

Strategy 10   Point of View

Directions:
Read the explanation, then complete the exercises.

A story is always told by someone. This person is called the narrator. The narrator may be someone who participates in the action of the story, or someone outside the action of the story. The narrator may have a limited range of knowledge, or may know everything there is to know about the story. The narrator may be reliable or unreliable. All of these factors go into what is called the story's **point of view.**

Stories can be told in the **first-person point of view.** In this case, the narrator is usually someone who was present or involved in the action of the story, and this person tells the story using the pronoun *I* to indicate personal involvement.

Stories can also be told in the **second-person point of view,** which is distinguished by the fact that the narrator speaks to the reader as *you,* and addresses the reader directly, as if they were speaking together.

The **third-person point of view** describes a narrator who is separate from the action and tells it from a greater distance than a first-person narrator would.

A narrator can be **omniscient,** knowing all the action of the story, even including what is going on in all the characters' minds and knowing what will happen in the end before it happens, or **limited** to knowledge of the perspective of only one character. When an author chooses a limited point of view, she or he is more likely to use devices like irony (see Strategy 3) to allow readers to know more than the character from whose point of view the story is told.

It is an essential point that the reader cannot assume that the narrator of a story is the author. Usually the narrator of a work of fiction is a persona created by the author for the purpose of relating the story.

1. Has the narrator mentioned anything in the story thus far that Jonas has not directly experienced?

2. Find three passages that show the narrator's access to Jonas's inner thoughts and feelings.

3. Does the narrator report anyone else's inner thoughts and feelings?

4. What seems to be the narrator's relationship to the events of the story?

5. From what point of view is the story told?

6. As you read, look for examples of irony that allow you to see beyond the point of view. You will find it valuable to skim chapters you have already read to find passages that you took at face value on first reading, but which in the light of information revealed later, turn out to be ironic.

Writer's Forum 4 Description

In a piece of descriptive writing, you let the readers know about the attributes of something so they can picture it in their mind's eye. You choose which features to mention based on what stands out among the physical properties and internal attributes of what you are describing, and these features will change depending on your topic. For example, in describing The Receiver's rooms, Lowry chose to focus on features such as "furniture," "practicality vs. beauty," and "books." When The Receiver describes the experience of a sled ride to convey the weight of the memories, he focuses on the "emotion," the "physical description" of the sled interacting with the snow, and the changing "role of the sledder."

Here are some questions to help you formulate your description:

- What is it that is being described?
- What are its attributes?
- How is it apprehended by the senses—how does it look, smell, taste, feel, sound?
- How does it relate to other things in its environment or context?
- How can it be described using answers to who, what, where, when, and how questions?
- What comparisons or contrasts can you make that will bring out its features?

The way you organize the information you will use can vary depending on what you are describing. You can organize your description from

- top to bottom
- front to back
- side to side
- inside and outside
- around the perimeter
- from the beginning to the end of its cycle or process

Source words that can help you express the relationship in space between parts of an object include

- above/below
- inside/outside
- around
- beside
- over/under
- nearby
- beneath/above
- to the right/left
- before/behind

Source words that can help you express concepts of similarity and difference if you use comparisons or contrasts include the following:

- also
- and
- as well as
- differ
- whereas
- however
- besides
- at the same time
- similarly
- while
- but
- on the contrary
- in addition
- too
- resemble
- conversely
- though
- on the other hand

Source words that can help you express sequence are

- first, second, etc.
- finally
- next
- afterwards
- then
- also

1. Write a description of part of the Assignment ceremony. Then write a description of Jonas's role as Receiver of Memory, as you understand it now. Afterwards, write a brief note on the differences in content and organization between your two descriptions.

Name _____

Vocabulary

Look at each group of words. Tell why it is important in the story.

1. meticulously, monitored, scrupulously

   _____

2. boyishness, buoyancy, precision, lapse

   _____

3. vibrant, gracious, benign

   _____

4. integrity, magnitude, spontaneously, collective

   _____

5. restriction, requisitioned, excruciating, diminished, throb, indescribable

   _____

6. slender, alcove, intricate, embossed

   _____

Essay Topics

1. What do you think the main conflict in the plot is going to be? Explain what led you to this conclusion.

2. What three questions would you most like to ask the current Receiver of Memory? Explain what you want to know and why.

3. How do you think Jonas's relationships with his friends will develop now? Explain why you think as you do.

4. Do you think there are any jobs in our society in which people feel justified in lying? Which jobs? What do you think about this?

5. How does Jonas compare with real eleven/twelve year olds you know? Is he "real" enough so that you find the characterization believable?

6. Where do you think the community is? Do you think it matters to the story? Explain why or why not.

7. What creates suspense in this story? Identify the techniques the author has used.

8. Do you like Jonas? Explain why you do or do not.

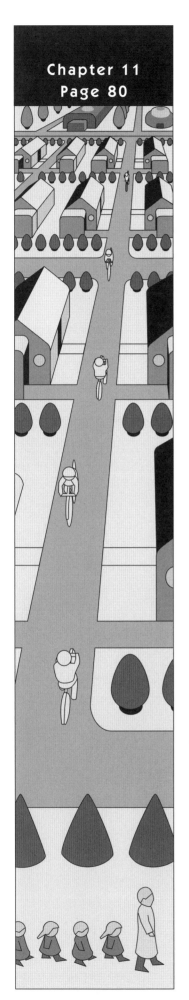

Chapter 11

Journal and Discussion Topics

1. Which senses are involved in Jonas's perception of the memories?
2. How is Jonas's understanding of the memories he receives different from his usual way of understanding things?
3. Have you ever understood something just by experiencing it without any explanation? Tell about it.
4. In speaking of the memory of sledding, Jonas says, "I took it from you!" Would you distinguish between taking and receiving in this situation? Explain.
5. At some point in the past, the community seems to have chosen a way of life that is referred to as Sameness. What kinds of experiences and hopes do you think led to this choice?
6. Why do you think The Receiver does not respond to Jonas's comment about understanding the pain of being the new Receiver?
7. Why do you think The Receiver looks sad at the end of the first day?
8. In what ways do we preserve memories in our society?
9. On page 75, the old man refers to himself as "The Receiver." On page 87, he refers to himself as "The Giver." What significance do you attach to this?
10. Characterize The Giver.

Vocabulary

intake: 80, what is taken in
frigid: 80, intensely cold
peppered: 80, showered or sprinkled
sensation: 81, feeling
whirling: 81, moving in a circle
torrent: 81, rush
perceived: 81, saw; was aware of
poised: 81, staying in readiness
descent: 81–82, downward motion
propelled: 82, provided power for
glee: 82, delighted; happiness

incline: 82, tilt
obstruction: 82, something in the way
unpredictable: 83, not able to be foretold
obsolete: 84, outdated
conveyance: 84, carrying; transporting
unwieldy: 84, awkward and complex
quizzically: 85, curiously or in a puzzled way
transmission: 86, communication
basking: 86, lying in a warm spot
crease: 86, fold
upholstered: 87, covered with fabric

Summary

At the same time feeling himself lying on the bed in the man's room with the man's hands on his back, and experiencing himself sitting poised on a sled at the top of a hill, Jonas is aware—first through touch, then taste, then sight, then sound—of snow and a sled ride down a hill. The experience is self-explanatory, with words coming into his mind to name the concepts he experiences—*snow, sled, hill, downhill, runners*. When it is done, Jonas is surprised, and the man is both tired and relieved of some of the weight of the memories, since he no longer has this one memory to carry. At first, Jonas feels as if he has stolen something, but the man explains that he has many other memories of sled rides and that he *gave* the memory to Jonas.

The man plans to transmit another memory, but Jonas interrupts, asking why snow, sleds, and hills are no longer present in the community. The man explains that lack of snow is due to Climate Control, one of the changes that accompanied the community's decision to choose Sameness. Jonas wishes snow and hills and sleds still existed and suggests that with his power, the man could have them returned. The man agrees that having them would be nice, but differentiates between what he has from his position—honor—and power, which he does not have. He then transmits a memory of sunshine, but without giving Jonas any idea of the memory content in advance. Jonas understands the word *sunshine* directly from his experience of the memory. This pleases the man, who sees that with Jonas's ability to learn quickly and to grasp concepts from experience, he will not need to explain much to Jonas.

Jonas enjoyed both transmitted memories but is confused, since the Chief Elder and the man both told him that his job will be painful. He tells the man that he is brave, and the man responds by offering him one more memory transmittal. In a memory that Jonas realizes exists in a different time frame than Jonas's real life, he experiences a memory of several hours in the sun that leads to a sunburn. Jonas says that this memory helps him understand what it means that the memories are painful, but the man doesn't respond to this comment. Instead, after a few moments, he tells Jonas that it is time to leave. Jonas thanks him, and then pauses to ask what he should call the man, who now seems extremely weary and sad. The man responds, "Call me The Giver."

Chapter 12

Journal and Discussion Topics

1. How does Jonas's answer to his mother's question about his sleep and dreams reveal a change in him?
2. What do you think is the significance (if any) of Jonas's dream? Explain.
3. What discovery is Jonas making about language and communication?
4. What do you imagine the change is that Jonas sees in Fiona's hair, and saw in the faces of the audience and in the apple?
5. What do you think would be different in the world if we had only one-generation memories?
6. Are your feelings about Sameness undergoing any change? Explain.
7. Imagine trying to describe the quality of color to someone who has never experienced it. What might you add to The Giver's explanation?
8. When The Giver tells Jonas, "It took me many years." (page 96), what does he mean?
9. How is The Giver adapting his training to fit Jonas?

Vocabulary

fretful: 88, upset
significant: 88, important
commerce: 89, buying and selling
industry: 89, manufacturing
technology: 89, technical processes
civil: 89, having to do with legal processes
abuzz: 89, filled with/communicating about
admonition: 89, warning
administrative: 90, having to do with supervising and/or managing
dietary: 90, food preparation, nutrition
occupational therapy: 90, activity that promotes healing or recovery
entirety: 90, complete being

energetic: 91, filled with energy
flustered: 91, confused and upset
phenomenon: 91, event or occurrence
fleeting: 93, passing quickly
impression: 93, indistinct experience
quality: 94, essential element or feature
distinctive: 94, noticeable; standing out
flesh: 94, skin
genetic: 95, having to do with inheritance through genes
kinks: 95, imperfections; problems
comprehend: 95, understand
relinquished: 95, let go of; gave up

Summary

The morning following his first training session, Jonas avoids a fully truthful communication for the first time, not giving a complete and direct answer to his mother's question about his dreams. Actually, he had dreamed the sled ride over and over, but with the sense of a destination to be reached farther beyond where the ride ended. At school, Jonas cannot speak of his training, and as he listens to his friends, he considers the inadequacy of language, no matter how precise, to convey what he has experienced.

Again, Jonas and Fiona ride to training together, but this time there are several moments of discomfort as Fiona describes her training experience and waits, expecting Jonas to reciprocate, but he doesn't. As they part, Jonas again has the experience that he now refers to as "seeing beyond," this time with Fiona's hair, which changes for a moment. The experience makes Jonas a minute late for his training, and he tells The Giver about it. The Giver thinks he understands (although his own initial experience of "beyond" was different), and to test his idea, he has Jonas lie down and tells him to recall the memory of the sled ride from the previous day. It is in this context that Jonas comes to understand that he now has the power to recall the memory himself, even though it goes back generations before his time. In the memory, he sees the same thing in the sled that he saw in the apple and in Fiona's hair. At The Giver's direction, he also finds the same quality in some of The Giver's books. The Giver explains to Jonas that what he is beginning to see is the color red, and then he tries to explain color to Jonas. He tells Jonas that he himself sees all the colors all the time, and that Jonas will too. Colors were given up when differences were ended at the time the community went to Sameness. He explains that there was a trade—letting go of certain things to gain control of others. Jonas bursts out that the trade-off was a mistake. The Giver responds that he has come to the same conclusion, but it has taken him a lot longer than it took Jonas. Recalling that they have much work to do, he resolves to help Jonas with color by giving him the memory of a rainbow.

Chapter 13

Journal and Discussion Topics

1. What does it mean that Jonas's life is no longer ordinary?
2. In Chapter 12, The Giver revealed that he agreed with Jonas about Sameness (page 96). Which of his statements in this chapter seem consistent with that? Which seem inconsistent? Explain.
3. Why do you think Jonas tries to share colors with Asher even though he thinks The Giver would have refused permission?
4. How did you react to the section about the elephants? What do you think happened to all the elephants in the world?
5. Why do you think Asher, Lily, and Father can't receive the memories Jonas tries to convey?
6. What do you think of the community's concept of family?
7. Explain what you think The Giver means when he says the memories *are* his life.
8. Why do you think The Giver doesn't just tell the Elders what he wants them to know?
9. What do you think The Giver means when he says, "without the memories, it's all meaningless" (page 105)? Do you agree with him? Explain.
10. Why does The Giver smile harshly when he refers to the honor of being The Receiver?
11. What do you think are the answers to Jonas's questions about Elsewhere (pages 106–107)?
12. What character traits does Jonas reveal in his comments on page 107?

Vocabulary

hueless: 97, without color
irrationally: 99, without reason
vibrance: 99, energy and liveliness
windswept: 99, exposed to wind
vast: 99, very large
sparse: 100, widely spaced; not thick
hack: 100, cut with repeated and irregular blows
perception: 100, sensory experience
mutilated: 100, damaged beyond repair
sinuous: 100, having many curves
skeptically: 101, with doubt

indifferently: 101, carelessly
exempted: 101, freed from following
array: 102, arrangement
successor: 104, person who follows another
vaguely: 104, without precision
assimilated: 104, incorporated into the mind
electrode: 105, thing that emits an electrical charge
disregarded: 105, ignored
embedded: 106, an integral/essential part
spanned: 106, extended across
altered: 106, changed

Summary

After weeks of training, Jonas is able to regularly catch glimpses of colors in ordinary life, although he realizes that his life is now beyond the ordinary. He is angry that he can't see the colors all the time, and complains that he wants choices, both for himself and for others. The Giver points out that people might make wrong choices, and Jonas concludes that while the choice of color might be innocuous, later choices, such as choosing a mate or a job, might turn out very badly, and that "we" have to protect people from wrong choices, because it's safer that way. The conversation does not ease Jonas's frustration, however, and he even tries, without permission and without success, to transmit color to Asher.

One day, Jonas receives a memory of a hot, dry land in which ivory hunters shoot an elephant and hack off its tusks. Jonas sees a second elephant approach, caress the body, cover it with leaves, and trumpet a cry of mourning.

At home, seeing Lily's comfort object, he tells her that elephants really existed once, but she doesn't believe him. He then tries to transmit to Lily and their father a memory of elephants, but he only succeeds in hurting Lily by squeezing her shoulder too hard.

One day, Jonas asks The Giver if he has a spouse. The Giver tells Jonas that he had a spouse who now lives with the childless adults. The Giver warns Jonas that if he has a spouse, it will be hard for him, because his spouse and children will be unable to share either his experiences or his books. He asks if Jonas understands that the memories ARE his life. Jonas is puzzled, because he thinks of life as doing. The Giver explains that his "doing" related to the memories is limited, because the Committee of Elders rarely calls for his counsel. He wishes they would consult them more, because there are things he wishes they would change, but he can only respond to their requests. Jonas doesn't see what the point of having a Receiver is if he is used so infrequently. The Giver explains the scope of The Receiver's role by telling Jonas what happened when the training of a new Receiver failed ten years earlier—all the memories of the new Receiver were released, and suddenly everyone in the community had access to them. The widespread suffering caused by the memories created a state of chaos that lessened only gradually. The Receiver's job is to experience the memories, including any pain that may accompany them, and gain the knowledge that goes with them on behalf of the community. The Giver reiterates that the memories are his life, and when Jonas interrupts to tell him about the chemistry of the brain, The Giver dismisses the explanation as unimportant. "Without the memories," he says, "it's all meaningless."

There are times when The Giver is so overwhelmed by the pain that he sends Jonas away without any training. One day after a day of no training, Jonas offers to take on some of The Giver's suffering to lessen his pain. The Giver accepts his offer, indicating that he has been trying to protect Jonas, and tells him that they will start with a hill and a sled.

Writer's Forum 5   Persuasion

Persuasive discourse attempts to change what the audience thinks, believes, or values, or to move the audience to take action. In most persuasive discourse, the writer or speaker states a position and then provides evidence or reasons that attempt to convince the audience to embrace that position. Look back at the conversation between Jonas and The Giver in the beginning of Chapter 13. This is an example of persuasion, but it is very subtle.

Writers and speakers use a variety of techniques to make their communications persuasive. Some of these techniques are logical and reasonable and accepted in our culture as examples of convincing argument. Other techniques that appeal to the audience's prejudices, or to instincts that most people would consider base (like greed), may be used, but are often seen as inappropriate. Appeals to the audience's emotions are considered acceptable in some cases but not in others, and must be used carefully. Here are some examples of valid techniques for persuasion:

- Follow the standards for discourse in your community—make sure that your approach is courteous and presented in an appropriate forum. Jonas respects the community demand for precise and accurate language when he corrects himself after calling Gabriel his brother.
- Tell the truth. If you cannot find convincing evidence, consider changing your point of view. Jonas changes his opinion that choice is important when he realizes the possible consequences of people making their own determinations about jobs and mates.
- Appeal to authority is a way to substantiate your claims. Make sure that the authority you cite is well respected. Usually when we talk about appealing to authority we mean a well-respected person or authoritative book. But when The Giver says that Gabriel "might make wrong choices," he may be appealing to the authority of experience, another kind of authority that carries a great deal of weight.
- Use specific details, such as statistics and other numerical data. If you use numbers or other facts, verify them carefully. You have a responsibility to present accurate information. Jonas does not use numbers, but he gives the specific example of Gabriel making a choice between a red and a yellow toy.
- Make your point in several different ways. This will help ensure that you have communicated clearly and may help reinforce your point. Jonas considers the consequences both of choosing a "wrong" mate and a "wrong" job.

Organization can be important in persuasion. Think carefully about the order in which you will present your evidence or arguments. Writers are often urged to put the most important reason first (or last), and then organize the other reasons in descending (or ascending) order of importance.

Knowing your audience is particularly important in persuasion. Knowing how their views differ from yours will show you what points you need to address. If you can anticipate their counter arguments, you can forestall them by showing why they either don't apply or are not valid for some other reason.

1. In a persuasive essay, attempt to convince Jonas that freedom to choose is worthwhile, despite the "wrong" choices that will be made. Use techniques from among those listed above.

Chapter 14

Journal and Discussion Topics

1. Jonas has to come to terms with the meaning of pain. Do you think we can find meaning in pain? Relate your experience to Jonas's.
2. Do you think it's better to share sorrows or for each person to try to bear his or her own pain? Explain your answer.
3. Can you think of a way that Jonas and The Giver could change the arrangement about memories in the community? Explain your ideas.
4. Why do you think one of a set of identical twins is always released?
5. What do you think are the answers to Jonas's questions on page 115?
6. How did you feel when you read about Larissa's release?
7. How did Jonas feel about giving Gabriel a memory?
8. Why do you think Jonas was able to transmit a memory to Gabriel, when he couldn't with Asher, Lily, or his father?
9. What do you think of Jonas's decision not to tell about transmitting a memory?

Vocabulary

skittered: 108, moved rapidly across a surface
jarred: 108, bumped
daub: 109, application of a sticky substance
unendurable: 110, unbearable
isolation: 110, being cut off from others
assuage: 110, lessen
distended: 111, swelled by internal pressure
unfulfilled: 112, unmet needs
ominous: 113, foreshadowing an evil or disastrous future
placidly: 114, calmly
dismay: 114, alarm
lull: 116, soothe or calm
billowing: 116, swelling
dimmer: 116, less clear and vivid
wisp: 117, a trace or hint

Summary

Jonas begins receiving a memory that is similar to his earlier sledding memory. But in this memory, the hill is icy, he loses control of the sled, and is thrown off, breaking his leg. Even after the memory is finished, the pain continues, and when Jonas asks The Giver for "relief-of-pain," The Giver says no and turns away.

Jonas limps home, circumvents his father's questions about how he's feeling, and goes to bed early. He realizes that his family has never felt pain, and he feels lonely and isolated in his experience. He dreams the memory repeatedly throughout the night. After this, there is pain in every training session, and Jonas is led to question why the two Receivers have to have these memories. The Giver explains that the memories supply wisdom that is necessary for giving appropriate advice to the Committee of Elders. For example, it was memories of hunger that led him to advise them not to increase the birthrate. Jonas suggests that it would be easier if the memories were shared, but The Giver responds that in that case, all people would be burdened and people don't want the burden. This, he says, is the reason why The Receiver has so much honor. Jonas still wants to change things, but neither he nor The Giver see any possibility for change.

The focus switches to Gabriel who is growing well but has trouble sleeping. Father and Mother discuss whether this isn't sufficient reason for him to be released. The discussion switches to a birth of twins that will take place soon. It seems that one of every set of identical twins is always released and that Father is the nurturer who is next in line to handle a release. Jonas imagines someone from Elsewhere coming to meet the released child, perhaps Larissa, who was recently released, but he realizes that the

Old would have a difficult time taking care of a newchild. Jonas suddenly has an idea and suggests that he could take care of Gabriel at night. His parents accept the idea, and the first time they try it, Gabe sleeps peacefully until the middle of the night. Jonas tries patting Gabe's back, but this doesn't quiet him, and Jonas falls into a reverie in which he recalls a memory The Giver had transmitted. Suddenly he realizes that the memory is becoming dimmer and recognizes that the memory is passing through his hand into Gabriel, who has suddenly calmed. He quickly withdraws his hand and stops the flow of the memory. Jonas returns to bed, but Gabriel wakes again toward morning and this time Jonas purposely gives him the rest of the memory. Gabriel falls back to sleep, and Jonas lies awake, thinking about the memory he has lost/given, and wondering whether or not he should tell The Giver about what has happened. He decides not to tell.

STRATEGY 11

Characterization Continuum

Directions: Read the explanation, then complete the exercises.

We often speak of **character traits** as absolutes—that is, characters either have them or not. So we might describe a character as thoughtful and gentle. This is useful for a start. But even a character that we recognize as thoughtful and gentle in general can be more or less gentle and more or less thoughtful, depending on the situation. Considering the variations in character traits can be the first step in taking a more realistic view of the complex thing we call character. We can consider character traits as existing on a continuum, a scale with opposite traits at the ends and a whole range of possible points in between. For example:

self-controlled — — — — — — — — — — overwhelmed

Think about The Giver: he is presented initially as a man who is in control not only of himself, but of the repository of knowledge of the community. He controls not only the memories of the community but also their transmission. Now look back at pages 105–106, where The Giver is unable to work with Jonas. He is overwhelmed by the memories and knowledge and pain that burden him. You can see that The Giver's trait of being in control is responsive to circumstances, and that to say The Giver is or isn't self-controlled would not come near to telling the whole story.

1. For each continuum, write a paragraph telling how the character(s) indicated move(s) along it during the course of the book.

   gullible — — — — — — — insightful (Jonas, the community)

   honest — — — — — — — deceptive (Jonas)

   follower/dependent — — — — leader/independent (The Giver, Jonas, Father)

2. Choose a single character and write a full-page description of his or her character traits. Explain how his or her behavior varies along each continuum that you identify. Use the information you have acquired so far, and add to your description as you read further in the book.

Chapter 15

Journal and Discussion Topics

1. How is Jonas now a Giver?
2. How does this chapter affect your view of whether it is better to share memories or bear them alone?
3. Do you think The Giver needs to ask Jonas's forgiveness? If you were Jonas, what would you have said in response to The Giver's request for forgiveness? Why?
4. How do you think Jonas will feel about The Giver and his Assignment now?

Vocabulary

contorted: 118, twisted
braced: 118, prepared
carnage: 119, corpses
spurt: 119, sudden forced gush
immobilized: 119, unable to move; paralyzed
splintery: 119, with lots of little sharp bits sticking out
surging: 119, rushing
trickled: 119, dripped slowly
imploring: 119, begging
grimy: 119, dirty

Summary

One day, arriving for training, Jonas sees that The Giver is in anguish. The Giver asks him to take some of the pain, and Jonas agrees to share the memory. The memory transmitted is of a battleground, covered with dying men and horses. A boy lying near Jonas begs him for water, and though Jonas feels that one of his arms is broken, he is able to reach his other arm across with a canteen and pour water into the young soldier's mouth. The boy drinks, and dies. Jonas lies there wounded and overcome by pain, listening to the cannon fire and smelling the decay. When the transmission is over, The Giver begs Jonas's forgiveness.

Writer's Forum 6   Diary Entries

In a **diary entry,** you record the important events of the day from your own point of view. Diaries may also link the present to the past or include hopes, dreams, or plans for the future.

Some parts of a diary might be rather objective, while others might be very personal and subjective. Diary writing is often informal—because people usually write diaries for themselves, they don't follow all the rules of grammar, punctuation, and usage. People may use words with private meanings, abbreviations, etc.

Diaries are not necessarily all your own words. Some people choose to quote others whose words they find helpful, interesting, or meaningful. Some people have a combination diary and scrapbook. Others draw in their diaries. Since a diary is personal, it can take many forms.

1. Choose a character from this book. Write four diary entries for that character. You may wish to write one for each of several chapters, or you may find your own way of deciding what to write about. Feel free to embellish and elaborate, while staying "in character."

Vocabulary

Look at each group of words. Tell why it is important in the story.

1. frigid, peppered, sensation, whirling, torrent, descent, glee _____

   _____

2. administrative, dietary, occupational therapy _____

   _____

3. windswept, hack, mutilated, sinuous _____

   _____

4. assuage, distended, unfulfilled _____

   _____

5. lull, billowing, dimmer, wisp _____

   _____

6. carnage, splintery, trickled, imploring, grimy _____

   _____

Essay Topics

1. What is your favorite moment in the story so far? Why do you like it best?

2. If you were writing this story, how would you end it? Describe the main events you would include in the rest of the plot.

3. You may have noticed that sometimes (but not always) the definite article (*the*) is capitalized in front of the words *Receiver* and *Giver*. I asked Lois Lowry through her publisher if these titles should always appear with a capital *The*. The answer was yes (phone conversation 1/12/98), and the places in the book where *the* is spelled with a lower case *t* will be corrected when the book is reprinted. What do you think is the significance of the capitalization?

4. Why do you think that not talking about his training is the most frustrating of Jonas's rules?

5. Do you think Jonas would prefer our society to his community? Why or why not?

6. The Giver defines his life as being the memories. How would you define your life?

7. Do you think it is important for children to know about brutality to animals and war? Why or why not?

Chapter 16

Journal and Discussion Topics

1. Why does Jonas go back to The Giver?
2. Why is the memory of the birthday party special to Jonas?
3. What clues helped you infer what the unnamed celebration was? When were you certain?
4. Compare the treatment of the Old in the community to their treatment in the family scene Jonas receives as a memory. Which shows more respect and caring in your opinion? Explain.
5. Regarding the community's method of caring for the Old, Jonas asks, "It seems to work pretty well that way, doesn't it?" to which The Giver replies, "It works" (page 125). What do you think of The Giver's response?
6. Do you agree with Jonas that living the way they did in the memory is dangerous? Why or why not?
7. Why did Jonas lie on page 127?
8. How has Jonas changed since he was an Eleven?
9. Why do you think Jonas confides in Gabriel?
10. What do you think of Jonas's decision to stop taking the pills?

Vocabulary

uneventful: 121, without excitement or notable incident
ecstatic: 122, filled with joy
solitude: 122, being alone
bearings: 122, relative position
pervaded: 122, filled

contentedly: 123, with satisfaction
luxuriating: 123, taking enormous pleasure
flushed: 126, red in the face
generalized: 127, without specific meaning
wholeheartedly: 127, with all one's being
optimistic: 128, hopeful

Summary

After receiving the memory of war, Jonas does not want to go back to training. He feels even more than before the unfairness of the situation—that he must relinquish his childhood and bear the enormous burden of pain in order to free the others. But he goes to The Giver each day, nevertheless. The Giver, responding to Jonas's pain, gives him many good memories. Among the most significant for Jonas are a birthday party for an individual child, which allows him to enjoy a celebration of uniqueness, and riding a horse, which allows him to sense the possibilities of relationships between humans and animals.

One day he asks The Giver what his favorite memory is, just so he can look forward to it, but The Giver shares it immediately. Jonas sees a room in winter during a Christmas celebration. He sees the pet dog, the gifts, and the presence of older people along with the young, and smells the meal cooking in the house. He learns the words *family, love,* and *grandparents.* Jonas contrasts the treatment of grandparents in the memory and in his community, and says of the community approach, "It seems to work pretty well that way, doesn't it?" But The Giver only answers, "It works." Jonas thinks aloud about the benefits of having grandparents in the home, and wishes that The Giver could be his grandparent. But he still speaks of the "old" way of living as dangerous.

When Jonas gets home, he asks his father and mother if they love him, and they laugh at him for his imprecision of language, telling him that the word *love* is meaningless. They say that they enjoy him and are proud of him. Although the memory of love is the most meaningful thing Jonas has

ever felt, when Mother asks if he understands why using the word *love* is inappropriate, he says, "yes"—his first direct lie to his parents.

Gabriel's crib has been returned to Jonas's room, because it's the only place that Gabriel sleeps well. That night, Jonas tells the sleeping newchild about his yearning and hope that things could be different—that their world could have colors, grandparents, shared memories (like those he now gives to Gabriel every night), and even love. The next morning, Jonas chooses not to take the pill for Stirrings—he throws it away.

Writer's Forum 7 **Personal Letter**

There are two main categories of letters that we usually speak of: business letters and **personal letters.** Business letters are formal: they include communications about commercial and legal dealings between and among organizations; consumer letters with requests, orders, or complaints; and letters of inquiry and application.

Personal letters are informal. Unlike business letters,

- they include only the date, not the return address in the **heading;**
- they do not include an **inside address;**
- the **salutation** ends with a comma, rather than a colon;
- each paragraph of the **body** is indented, not put in block form;
- the **closing** is friendly and personal and followed by a comma;
- they are usually handwritten rather than typed.

_____	Date
_____,	Salutation
_____	Body with indented paragraphs
_____,	Closing, followed by comma
	Handwritten signature

Personal letters include thank-you letters, invitations, pen-pal letters, and letters to keep in touch with friends who are absent.

1. Write a letter to Jonas about what love means to you. Tell him why it would or wouldn't, in your opinion, be worthwhile to have it in his community. Tell him what steps he could take to try to foster love, if he were to try and restore it.

Chapter 17

Journal and Discussion Topics
1. What process led you to understand the first sentence of Chapter 17?
2. What changes have the memories brought about in Jonas?
3. How is the game of war a turning point in Jonas's experience?
4. Why does Jonas refuse Fiona's invitation?
5. What does Father's certainty about the birthday of the twins reveal about how births are handled in the community?
6. Everyone seems to accept the idea of releasing a twin simply because it's a twin in a matter of fact way. How do you feel about this attitude?

Vocabulary
permeated: 131, filled
passionately: 132, with powerful emotion
staggered: 132, to move unsteadily; to sway or totter forward
freakish: 133, abnormal; unusual and weird
postures: 133, body positions
horde: 133, large crowd

Summary
Greeted one morning by the announcement of an unexpected holiday, Jonas rides off on his bike to look for Asher. As he rides, he is conscious of his heightened feelings, due both to the memories and to his not taking the pills for four weeks. In the light of his new awareness, he reviews and reinterprets the community's understanding of those feelings that the citizens constantly review and analyze, finding those "feelings" to be shallow and limited.

Suddenly, Jonas spots Asher's bike and sees his friends playing a game of "good guys and bad guys" that has up until now had no name. The children make sounds of weapons, yell responses like, "you got me," or "you're hit," and fall to the ground grinning and giggling. But now, for the first time, Jonas recognizes what they're doing as a game of war, and horrified, he stands in their midst, trying not to cry. All the children except Asher and Fiona leave. Fiona asks what's wrong, while Asher accuses Jonas of ruining their game. Jonas tries to explain what's wrong with the game, but Asher only responds with the formulaic community apology, with no understanding. Fiona invites Jonas to ride along the river, but he declines and sits by himself, realizing that without the memories, his friends can neither understand nor feel true love. And he feels that he cannot change anything.

At home, Jonas is cheered by Gabriel's antics, but soon the talk turns to the birth of the identical twins that will occur the following day. Jonas asks if his father takes the twin Elsewhere, but Father says he just cleans the newchild, performs a ceremony of release, and waves goodbye. Jonas asks again about what happens next—whether someone comes from Elsewhere to get the child, and his father says, "that's right." Lily, thinking about this, makes up a story about identical twins who are separated in this way are unwittingly given the same name, and meet on a school field trip where they get mixed up. Then, after a break, she suggests another scenario in which it turns out that everyone in the community is a twin. Father ends the discussion by sending Lily to bed.

Strategy 12   Inferencing

Directions: Read the explanation, then complete the exercises.

Inferencing is a frequent activity, but it has at least two meanings. Sometimes it means "figuring something out from the facts presented in a text." For the sake of clarity, we're going to call this **drawing a conclusion.** Other times, however, it means "bringing outside knowledge to bear on the facts in the text." This is what we're going to refer to as inferencing here. Making inferences is essential to comprehension of a text, because writers do not tell everything. In fact, writers depend on readers to interpret and construe, to gather information or details from different parts of the books, apply their own knowledge and thought, and make leaps of understanding.

Inferencing goes on in life, not just in reading, and in the lives of fictional characters as well. Lowry shows Jonas making an inference in Chapter 17. At the top of page 133, Jonas observes the game his friends are playing, and using the knowledge gained from a memory The Giver has shared with him, interprets it as a game of war. As a reader, you might infer from this incident, along with others in your experience, the value of memory in helping us find meaning in the actions of our lives.

Inferencing is a hard skill to teach. Because it involves putting together text from different parts in the book and bringing outside knowledge to bear on it, it is hard to describe exactly how to DO it. Part of it depends on making links among ideas, descriptions, analyses, and actions in different parts of the text. An active reader who is engaged in looking for the themes and meaning of a work will usually notice a lot of these links. Did you notice that after referring to Gabriel's and Jonas's pale eyes in 4 paragraphs in Chapter 3 (pages 20–21 and 25), and mentioning that The Receiver has pale eyes in Chapter 8 (page 61), that in Chapter 10 (page 75), the pale eyes of The Receiver and Jonas are mentioned again? What can you infer from this? Bringing your knowledge that repetition of a topic is a way of indicating importance, you could infer that pale or light eyes are a physical expression of an inner disposition and ability to a) give and receive memories, b) acquire wisdom, and c) feel deeply, and that Lowry wants you to recognize that Gabriel, in spite of his slow development, is a person with a special gift that can be of enormous value to the community.

1. Explain the inference that led Jonas to sigh at the top of page 135.

2. How and why did Jonas conclude that "such times had been taken from him now" (page 135)?

3. Jonas infers that, "he can change nothing" (page 135). Do you infer the same? Explain.

Chapter 18

Journal and Discussion Topics

1. What do you think led Jonas to bring up the topic of release?
2. What do you gather from the fact that after nearly a year, Jonas still apologizes for imprecision, interrupting, and rudeness, despite The Giver's assurances that he needn't?
3. Why do you think Jonas refers so often to the honor of his assignment?
4. Contrast The Giver's feelings for Jonas with Mother's and Father's feelings for Jonas.
5. How do you interpret Jonas's reaction to The Giver's telling about the first painful memory he gave Rosemary?
6. When The Giver looks at Jonas imploringly, what does he want?
7. What do you think of The Giver's statement, "Memories are *forever*"?
8. What do you think The Giver is thinking about on the bottom of page 144, when the narrator says he is "obviously thinking"?

Vocabulary

dejected: 139, sad and depressed
despite: 139, in spite of
self-possessed: 140, sure of oneself
ruefully: 141, sadly; with sorrow

luminous: 141, seeming brightly lit from within
inflict: 142, to impose something burdensome
devastated: 144, destroyed
lighthearted: 145, carefree and happy

Summary

Jonas arrives at The Giver's the following day with the topic of release on his mind, and he asks if The Giver ever considers the matter. The Giver says that he thinks about his own release when he's in pain, but that since the failure of ten years before, the rules have been changed to prohibit the release of a Receiver until the next Receiver is trained. Jonas asks to be told what happened.

The Giver describes her, and at Jonas's request, tells that her name was Rosemary. He relates that she was eager, that he explained things as well as he could, and that he loved Rosemary. He adds that he loves Jonas too. The Giver began by transmitting happy memories, but when she asked for the painful ones, he gave her one of loneliness, and she was in shock. They continued, but one day after training, Rosemary kissed The Giver's cheek, went to the Chief Elder, and asked for release. At that time there was no rule against it, so her request had to be granted, and The Giver never saw her again.

Jonas feels that the failure doesn't seem so terrible, and although he knows he can't be released, he wonders what would happen if there was an accident and he died, so that the memories that The Giver had already passed on to him were lost. The Giver explains that the memories wouldn't be lost; as happened when Rosemary was released, the memories would come back to the people (the way they used to be shared with everyone), because memories are forever. When Rosemary was released, the memories she had received and their attendant feelings overwhelmed the people of the community. The Giver reflects that if Jonas were lost, the people would once again have all the memories that he had acquired; the narrator comments that The Giver was obviously thinking, leaving the implication that he has gotten some idea from this reflection. The conversation continues as they consider what would happen if Jonas were lost, with The Giver suggesting that were this to occur, perhaps he could help the whole community with the memories in the same way that he is helping Jonas.

Chapter 19

Journal and Discussion Topics

1. What do you think The Giver means when he says, "I wish they wouldn't do that" (page 146)? Why do you think he feels as he does?
2. What do you think of Jonas's explanation of why the twin is being released?
3. What effect did Jonas's use of the word *comfy* instead of *comfortable* have on you?
4. When you first read The Giver's statement, "I think you should" (page 147), what did you think his reason was for suggesting so strongly that Jonas watch?
5. Now that you've finished Chapter 19, is your interpretation of "He was astonished and delighted" (page 147) different? Your interpretation of "That's the special voice he uses with Gabriel" at the top of page 149?
6. What foreshadows the knowledge Jonas receives in this chapter?
7. When did you realize what release means? What clues helped you come to that conclusion?
8. On page 143 in Chapter 18, the narrator indicated that Jonas didn't think that the failure with Rosemary was "such a terrible thing, after all." What do you think Jonas thinks now?
9. How would you define bravery?
10. What do you think Jonas will do now?

Vocabulary

syringe: 149, instrument for injecting fluids into the body
pulsed: 149, throbbed rhythmically due to contractions of the heart
plunger: 149, the part of a syringe that is pushed to move the fluid out

Summary

Jonas, glancing at the clock, apologizes for wasting time, and explains that release was on his mind because of the identical twin whom his father released that morning. The Giver says cryptically, "I wish they wouldn't do that." Jonas facilely dismisses this comment and then adds that he wishes he could have watched. The Giver tells Jonas that he can, since the ceremony has been recorded, and says that he thinks Jonas should. They begin to watch the tape, and Jonas responds to what he sees, but The Giver shushes him. They see Jonas's father and another Nurturer bring in the two babies and weigh them. The smaller of the two (by six ounces) is left with Jonas's father, and when Jonas begins to speak again, The Giver again tells him to be quiet. They watch as his father fills a syringe and injects it into the newchild's forehead. The newchild jerks around for a moment, then his head falls to the side and he is still. Jonas remembers the soldier who died in the memory of warfare and realizes that his father has killed the newchild. Father puts the body into a carton and places it in the trash, saying a cheery goodbye. The tape ends, and The Giver begins to speak. He tells of watching the tape of Rosemary's release: how they brought in the syringe and how she chose to inject herself, and he was unable to watch. Jonas feels that he is about to scream.

Strategy 13   Rereading a Book

*Directions:
Read the explanation, then complete the exercises.*

Think of a book you've known for a while and read at least twice. How does your understanding of this book differ from the way you understand a book you've read only once?

- Do you remember details better?
- Do you remember the sequence of events better?
- Have you memorized parts of it?
- Can you imagine the characters in another setting?
- Do you return to the book when you feel a certain way or want to feel a certain way?
- Do you feel that all the parts of the book fit together to form a whole integrated experience?

Authors and critics alike suggest that reading fiction should be experiential. Novelist Joseph Conrad wrote, "My task, which I am trying to achieve, is, by the power of the written word, to make you hear, to make you feel—it is before all, to make you see. That, and no more, but it is everything." Janet Burroway, a writing instructor elaborates: "Written words are . . . at two removes from experience. . . . They are transmitted first to the mind, where they must be translated into images. . . . What it means is that . . . [the] fiction writer [must] focus attention, not on the words, which are inert, nor on the thoughts these words produce, but through these to felt experience, where the vitality of understanding lies." In other words, we don't read literature for information; we read it in order to pass through (in our minds) the sequence of events the author proposes, allowing our minds and hearts to respond to these events.

But all of this doesn't happen without the extended and complex act that we call reading. And in our first reading of a text, we cannot give ourselves fully to experiencing the story because we have to:

- recognize black marks on the paper as letters and words
- process the words in groups to construct meaning and figure out how paragraphs and ideas are connected
- relate the perceived meaning to what we already know about stories in general, stories of the same genre as the one we're reading, earlier information from this particular story, etc.
- create in our minds the world of the story
- apply prior knowledge of facts, experiences, other stories, ideas, feelings, sensory data, etc., to help us understand what we have read
- try to recollect a new sequence of events and many facts and details
- fill gaps left by the text (no text tells absolutely everything that happened) with our own elaborations

Considering the enormous investment of energy required to read, author Vladimir Nabokov said, "one cannot *read* a book: one can only reread it. . . . When we read a book for the first time the very process of laboriously moving our eyes from left to right, line after line, page after page, this complicated physical work upon the book, the very process of learning in terms of space and time what the book is about, this stands between us and artistic appreciation. . . . In reading a book, we must have time to acquaint ourselves with it. We have no physical organ (as we have the eye in regard to a painting) that takes in the whole picture and then can enjoy its details. But at a second, or third, or fourth reading we do, in a sense, behave towards a book as we do towards a painting."

Rereading is also important when we want to clarify, re-experience, or check on our understanding of a link between different parts of a book.

Think about the events of Chapter 19. Did you remember, as you were reading, that Jonas's father had described the release of the twin a few pages earlier in Chapter 17 (pages 136–137)? Do you think Jonas remembered his father's words? Did you reread that description and compare it with the reality shown in the tape? This is the kind of situation in which rereading is important even before you've finished the story for the first time. The release of the twin is a crucial moment in the book, and in order for you to understand its significance, both to Jonas and to the story, you need to be thoroughly aware of the levels of irony, which depend on having the earlier passage in mind when you read.

1. Reread pages 136–137 and all of Chapter 19. Point out the ironies in Chapter 19. Identify which ones you only noticed upon rereading.

Strat.13, cont.

Chapter 20

Journal and Discussion Topics

1. What do you think The Giver means when he says, *"They know nothing"*? Do you agree? Explain.
2. How do you feel about Fiona now?
3. Do you agree now with the statement that "memories need to be shared" (page 154)? Explain why you do or do not.
4. What do you think The Giver has in mind when he says, "there might be a way" (page 155)?
5. Now what do you think pale eyes signify? Explain how you came to this conclusion.
6. Why do you think Jonas says, "You and I don't need to *care* about the rest of them" (pages 156–157)? Why does he hang his head afterwards?
7. How did you feel when you read that The Giver could no longer see colors?
8. Why can Jonas lie easily now?
9. Why does the day of the Ceremony seem like an ideal time for Jonas to leave the community?
10. What was the impact on you of the first direct statement of love in Jonas's life (page 162)?
11. How did your ideas change when you learned that Rosemary was The Giver's daughter?

Vocabulary

empowered: 153, gave power to
emphatically: 157, with emphasis
maintenance: 158, upkeep
mounting: 159, getting up on

disrupted: 161, disturbed
solace: 161, comfort
stride: 161, walk with long, confident steps

Summary

Jonas sobs uncontrollably, but obeys when The Giver tells him to be quiet so that he can notify Jonas's family unit that he will be keeping him overnight for additional training (actually so that Jonas does not need to go home). Jonas sarcastically attacks the community members who are involved in releases, but The Giver interrupts him, reminding him that they can't help it, because they do not have the memories, and thus know and feel nothing. Even Jonas's father only lied to Jonas because he was told to, The Giver tells him. Jonas asks if The Giver has lied to him, and The Giver tells him that he could have, but he has not. Then Jonas asks if all releases are the same, and The Giver says yes. Jonas is concerned about how Fiona will react when she finds out, because she loves the Old, but The Giver responds that Fiona already does releases and is very efficient because she has no feelings. Jonas can only respond that he can't return, and asks what he should do. The Giver responds, practically, that they will eat, leading Jonas to ask sarcastically if they'll share feelings after the meal as is the required custom in the community. The Giver points out that the two of them are the only ones in the community who have feelings, and that they have been REALLY sharing them for nearly a year.

The Giver continues, saying that after dinner they will make a plan, and Jonas voices his feeling that there is nothing they can do. The Giver says that the greatest burden of being Receiver is not the pain of the memories, but the loneliness, because memories need to be shared. And he tells Jonas that Jonas has given him an idea about how things could change.

The narration breaks and continues later that night. The plan is only barely possible, and if it fails it is likely that Jonas will be killed. They plan that Jonas will leave the community, releasing the memories and forcing the community to bear them, giving the others a chance to acquire wisdom and feelings. The Giver will stay behind to help them. Jonas begs The Giver to come with him and says, "you and I don't need to *care* about the rest of them," but he is immediately ashamed of the sentiment and knows that it isn't true. The Giver admits that he can no longer see colors, but he still has the ability that he began with—hearing beyond: The Giver can hear music. He says he will give some to Jonas before Jonas leaves, but Jonas says firmly that he wants The Giver to have that to keep.

Jonas returns home, and he and his father exchange lies about their activities on the previous day. Jonas goes to school, but during his lessons, he is actually reviewing the plan in his mind. For two weeks, The Giver will concentrate on giving Jonas memories filled with courage and strength. Then, on the night before the Ceremony, Jonas will sneak away from his dwelling, leaving a note for his parents saying he will be back for the Ceremony, hide a bicycle and a change of clothing by the riverbank, and go to The Giver's dwelling. The Giver will order a vehicle and, with Jonas and a supply of food hiding in the storage area, leave the community and travel the first leg of the escape journey. In the meantime, Jonas not having returned, his parents will go to the Ceremony without him, assuming he is with Asher or The Giver, and Jonas's friends thinking he is with his family unit. By the end of the Ceremony, when Jonas's absence has become apparent, the bicycle and clothing will have been discovered, and The Giver will have returned. The Giver will then come into the Auditorium to lead the people in the Ceremony of Loss for Jonas and to begin helping them to bear the memories.

Jonas recalls the end of the planning session, in which The Giver thanked him for providing the inspiration for the plan. Jonas, having finally accepted that The Giver will not come with him, asks whether the Giver wants to be with him, and for the first time in the book, there is a direct statement of love as The Giver says, "I love you, Jonas." But he goes on to say that when his work is done, he wants to be with his daughter. Jonas is surprised, because The Giver never told him that he'd had a daughter. The Giver smiles and replies that her name was Rosemary.

Writer's Forum 8   Reflection

A **reflection** could be compared to a written meditation on a subject. Less formal than an essay, a reflection entails letting your thoughts flow around an open-ended subject, and recording your thoughts and insights without too much shaping in the writing process. Thus a reflection is more spontaneous and may be less organized than an essay. It is more a record of what went on in your mind and less a showpiece prepared for others to see.

1. Reflect on the end of Chapter 19. Record your reflections after considering the following aspects.
   - Jonas's previous opinion of his father (remember Father's treament of Gabriel and Lily)
   - Jonas's responses to The Giver's comments throughout the chapter
   - All the details you now know about the story of Rosemary
   - The release of Roberto
   - Jonas's previous opinion of and feelings about Fiona
   - What Jonas will do now and how he will face his father

Strategy 14

Theme

Directions: Read the explanation, then complete the exercises.

The **theme** of a story might be thought of as the story's point or its message. A theme is usually a generalization about life or human behavior or values, true, but not a truism—the author's insight into the way things are that s/he wants to share with readers. Theme is an important part of a story's meaning and is developed throughout the story. And it is important to note that a story can have multiple themes and meanings.

The message of a story is always shaped by the author's intention and purpose. Besides patterns in the story (which often point to the theme), there are certain parts of a story that often refer to the theme: the title, the beginning, and the very end. An important character's first and final words or thoughts are also likely to carry powerful indications of theme.

A persuasive or didactic piece of writing (such as a fable) might have an explicit moral—a clear statement of theme. Such a statement can clearly convey the author's idea of what the story means, while limiting interpretation of the piece on the part of the reader. However, a piece of writing that was written with experience or aesthetic response in mind is more open to interpretation. Certainly the author may have a theme or themes in mind, but the readers bring their own understandings, and in this case different readers may legitimately find different meanings based on patterns and messages in the text combined with their own interpretations and insights. But we seek for a balance between what is in the text and what the reader brings to the text.

In a story such as *The Giver*, which deals with complex issues, you will likely find multiple themes. But also try looking for a single, over-arching theme.

1. State the theme or themes you find as you continue reading the story. Explain how you concluded that these statements are thematic. When you have completed the story, review your answer, modifying it in the light of new evidence.

Writer's Forum 9   Essay

Just as a fiction writer may develop a story around a central theme, an essayist develops an **essay** around a central idea, contention, or proposition. Every paragraph and sentence of an essay contributes to conveying this central thought to readers. This makes an essay different from a reflection, a diary entry, or a personal letter, all of which may be free-flowing and do not require the kind of unity that an essay needs.

There is not just one type of essay. Your central idea, when you write an essay about a story, can relate to a number of different aspects of the story. You could write an essay about characterization, about theme, about point of view, or about the effectiveness of certain literary techniques the writer used in creating the story, to name some examples.

An essay usually begins with a statement of the central idea you wish to convey. This is sometimes called the **thesis sentence.** The following paragraphs, organized in an order that makes sense for the particular idea you are developing, support the central idea, referring back to it as necessary. These paragraphs will often contain examples and quotations from the text. The final paragraph often summarizes the evidence and restates the central idea. The title you choose for your essay should also relate to your central idea.

The organization of the body of the essay will vary depending on the topic. Sometimes you may want to move chronologically through the story. For certain topics, you might want to move chronologically through the development of your ideas or impressions as you were reading. If your essay is persuasive, you might use order of importance, beginning with the most or least important reason, and moving toward the opposite end of the spectrum. In a compare and contrast essay, you would alternate between topics, either moving back and forth repeatedly from one to the other, or discussing one, and then discussing the other.

1. Write an essay about the theme or themes you found in *The Giver*. Use an appropriate organizational strategy. Give your essay a title.

Name _____

Vocabulary

Look at each group of words. Tell why it is important in the story.

1. pervaded, contentedly, luxuriating_____
_____

2. staggered. freakish, postures, horde _____
_____

3. ruefully, luminous, inflict, devastated _____
_____

4. syringe, pulsed, plunger _____
_____

5. disrupted, solace, stride_____
_____

Essay Topics

1. What do birthday parties mean to you? How do you think it would be different if everyone in your grade had a birthday celebrated on the same day at a public ceremony?

2. Rewrite the scene in which Jonas discovers the meaning of love using a different kind of memory. Be sure to include details that communicate the emotion and commitment of love effectively.

3. What do you think Gabriel will be like when he grows up? Explain why you think as you do.

4. What differences do you see between adoption as it is practiced in our country and family life in the community?

5. Why do you think Rosemary chose release?

6. What did The Giver learn from what happened to Rosemary?

7. How do you interpret the cover of the book now?

Chapter 21

Journal and Discussion Topics

1. When you first read that the plans made by The Giver and Jonas had fallen apart, what did you imagine had happened?
2. Do you think that The Giver knows that Jonas said goodbye (page 164)? On what do you base your conclusion?
3. How does the description of Jonas's evening meal with his family contrast with the description of Jonas's escape?
4. How did you react to the plan to release Gabe?
5. Why was Jonas interested in the scheduled date of Gabriel's release?
6. How do you feel about Father now?
7. In the paragraph after the break on page 165, how has Jonas's understanding of the community changed since the beginning of the book?
8. Under what circumstances would you consider taking leftover food a serious problem? Explain your response.
9. What do you think happened in the community the day that Jonas left? What do you think The Giver did?
10. Why do you think the planes stopped?

Vocabulary

stealthily: 163, secretly; to avoid notice
frazzled: 164, emotionally worn out
condemned: 165, pronounced guilty
languid: 166, lacking energy or spirit
hypnotically: 166, causing sleepiness
outlying: 166, lying on the outskirts of

rutted: 167, with pits or furrows, uneven
augmented: 168, added to
taut: 168, tense; tight
foliage: 169, leaves
vigilant: 170, watchful; alert to danger
haphazard: 170, not carefully planned

Summary

As Jonas reviews the plan, he assures himself of its possibilities, but the plan is not carried out—Jonas has to flee that very night. He has to leave earlier in the night than planned, when work crews are still present, and he cannot even stop to let The Giver know of the change in plans. As he crosses the bridge that separates the community from everything else, he is surprised at his lack of feeling about the community, and saddened by leaving The Giver. He tries to call back a goodbye in his mind, hoping that The Giver's capacity for hearing beyond will allow him to recognize the call.

The narration flashes back to reveal the motivation for Jonas's sudden departure. At dinner that night, Father had casually mentioned that it was Gabe's last night with the family. Gabe had spent a night at the Nurturing Center and slept very poorly, leading the Nurturers, including Father, to vote for Gabe's release. Lily, Mother, and Father agree they had tried hard to make things work out for Gabe. Jonas only asks quietly when Gabe will be released. Father answers that the release will take place early the following day.

The narration returns to Jonas's flight, and his review of the rules he has broken: leaving a dwelling at night, taking food from the community, stealing his father's bicycle because he needed the one with the child seat—and taking Gabe. Gabe, prepared by Jonas's transmission of a quieting memory, is sleeping soundly in the seat. Jonas rides through the night, stopping in a meadow in the morning, letting Gabe out of the seat, and feeding them both. Jonas needs to sleep even though Gabe has just awakened, so he gives Gabe a memory of exhaustion, and they both sleep.

For many days, search planes seek them, and although Jonas knows the pilots can't see color, he is concerned that they will be able to sense the heat of the two fugitives. He uses memories of snow to keep himself and Gabe cold to elude detection. Jonas begins to feel the memories weakening, and senses that they are beginning to leave him to return to the community. After awhile, the planes appear less frequently, and finally they do not appear for twenty-four hours.

STRATEGY 15   Narration

*Directions:
Read the explanation, then complete the exercises.*

We discussed in Strategy 10, Point of View, that the narrator in fiction is usually not the voice of the author. But the author's opinions and ideas are somehow present in the book. How does this work?

The author's views are communicated to us in a variety of ways. The ending of a work of fiction is one important way. How do things end up? What is/are the theme(s) of the work? These are "messages" to us from the author.

But the method we're going to focus on now is the author's communication through the characters. Wayne Booth, a professor of English, wrote in his book *The Rhetoric of Fiction* that "The author is present in every speech given by any character who has had conferred upon him, in whatever manner, the badge of reliability" (page 18).

How do we know whether a character is reliable? Consider how we are introduced to Jonas. Look back at the second sentence of the book. The word *no* is clearly a thought in Jonas's mind, not the narrator's comment. But it is not put in quotation marks, nor is it attributed. This shows readers that the narration is being presented from Jonas's vantage point. We see what Jonas sees. We also learn, from the next sentence, that Jonas tries to be very precise about his thought and his communication. On page 3, the narrator tells us directly, "Jonas was careful about language," and this supports what we have seen. You may have heard the adage that writers should "show, not just tell"—here, the telling supports the showing.

But as we sense that not everything is as wonderful as it seems in this orderly community (which some readers may do by page 2 as they read about the incident of the plane), we may begin to realize that Jonas does not understand everything that is happening in the community. One clue that his understanding is limited comes simply from the fact that he is a child, which most readers have probably surmised by page 2 or 3, and on page 9 we are given the information we need to figure out that he is eleven years old. Another clue is that his opinions begin to change, and he begins to question the system. As he matures, his views become more and more reliable.

1. Do this exercise after you finish reading the book, but read the instructions now so you can look for evidence as you read. It could be claimed that by the end of the book, we can believe anything Jonas says or thinks. Write a brief essay in which you support or discount this view. If you support it, note the last thing that Jonas says or thinks in the story that you think was unreliable and explain what changed after that. If you discount it, point out the instances in the final chapters that demonstrate Jonas's lack of reliability. Explain why it is or is not, in your view, essential that we accept Jonas as reliable in order to interpret the ending of the book.

Chapter 22

Journal and Discussion Topics

1. What kind of animal do you think Jonas sees but can't identify on page 172?
2. What incongruous feelings did Jonas have on pages 171–172?
3. If Jonas and Gabriel starve, will their venture have been worth it in your opinion? Explain.
4. Why does the text say, "he had made the wrong [choice]" (page 174), and a few lines later say, "there had not really been a choice," which seems to contradict the first statement.
5. What could have brought Jonas to the point where he would cry for Gabriel, but not for himself?
6. What do you think will happen next?

Vocabulary

jolted: 171, moved sharply by a sudden blow
perils: 171, dangers
wincing: 171, shrinking involuntarily due to pain
gullies: 171, trenches created by running water
exquisite: 172, flawlessly beautiful
relentless: 172, persistent
cultivated: 172, planted with crops
makeshift: 173, a substitute—often not a very good one
tantalizing: 173, desirable and unreachable
lush: 173, very pleasing to the senses
yearned: 174, longed

Summary

Farther away from the community, the roads are uneven, and one night Jonas falls from his bike, twisting his ankle and scraping his knees. He decides to try riding in daylight. The landscape shows less and less evidence of Sameness. They see forests and streams, birds, deer, and a squirrel, wildflowers, and fish. Past the area of cultivated fields, they find food hard to come by. Jonas improvises a net from Gabriel's blanket and catches some fish. Jonas's memories of hunger blend with this new reality. He uses memories to satiate his hunger, and when this proves unsatisfactory, thinks briefly that he has made a mistake in choosing to leave. But recalling that staying in the community was starvation of another kind, and that Gabe would have died, he is again reconciled to his choice. As the season changes, the weather grows cold and wet, adding to their discomfort. Gabriel cries in his hunger, and Jonas cries because he is afraid that he cannot save Gabriel, no longer caring about saving himself.

Chapter 23

Journal and Discussion Topics

1. Have you ever had an experience like Jonas's of feeling something (like his feeling that Elsewhere is near despite his having no concrete evidence) that your senses did not support? Did you believe the feeling or the "facts" your senses presented to you? Explain.
2. What did you think would happen or what did you think Jonas would do when the bicycle couldn't go any further?
3. Who are The Giver and The Receiver now? How might this change as time goes on? Explain.
4. How does the content of Jonas's memories change as he approaches the summit of the hill?
5. What does it mean that Jonas found "a memory of his own"?
6. What do you think awaited Jonas and Gabriel at the end of the sled ride?
7. Do you think Jonas really heard music behind or only an echo? Explain your reasoning.

Vocabulary

blurred: 175, not seen clearly; appearing with fuzzy edges
loomed: 176, came into sight indistinctly and seemingly very large
imperceptibly: 176, without being noticed
trudged: 177, walked steadily but with difficulty
lethargy: 177, state of inactivity and lack of commitment
resignation: 177, acceptance without resistance
impeded: 177, slowed in progress by an obstacle
summit: 178, peak
recollection: 178, memory
incision: 179, cut

Summary

Jonas's internal certainty that there is a destination that he is approaching strengthens, although there is nothing in the external world to support this assumption. But he is afraid they will never reach the destination, especially as the weather gets even colder, the snow begins, and Gabriel is miserable: tired, hungry, cold, and dirty. Approaching a steep hill in deep snow, Jonas is forced to abandon the bike, and despite his flagging strength, determines to climb the hill. The memories have faded, but he tries to transmit a memory of warmth to himself and Gabe, and for a moment they are both warm as Jonas begins the ascent. Several times he pauses in the difficult climb to warm them, but the warmth lasts only a brief time. Toward the end of the climb, Jonas begins to feel unaccountably happy, recalling his own pleasant times with his friends, and remembering The Giver. When they reach the summit, Jonas remembers the place from his own memory, and he finds the sled that he knew was waiting. The destination that he sensed first in his dreams, he is now certain of. And then he sees lights and recognizes them as the lights from the indoor tree that he saw in the memory of love. Suddenly he realizes that there are people waiting for him and Gabe, and he hears singing—the first music in his life. And behind him he hears music, too, or possibly only an echo.

STRATEGY 16   Dystopias

Directions: Read the explanation, then complete the exercises.

Utopias are attempts to formulate ideal societies that deliver us from the social, political, and economic turmoil we experience. Some utopias have been attempted in the real world when people chose a place and tried to create a community in which their ideal could become a reality. All such attempts have failed in one way or another. Other utopias appear in literature.

Utopia means "no place" in Greek, and the term was first used by Sir Thomas More in his book of that name, which showed a perfect society on an imaginary island. Since the publication of that book in 1516, the word *utopian* has been used to describe a work of literature in which an ideal society is presented.

Some writers have satirized the utopia, in a genre called antiutopia or **dystopia** (from the Greek meaning "bad or impaired place"). Dystopias show dehumanized rather than ideal societies, but like utopias, they focus on contemporary problems.

1. Do you think it is justifiable to classify *The Giver* as a dystopia? Why or why not?

2. Do you think that Lowry is criticizing our society? If so, what evils or ills of contemporary society do you think Lowry is addressing? If not, what do you think her purpose is?

3. Do you think that *The Giver* is a call to social action? If so, how? If not, why not?

Extending a Story
Writer's Forum 10

The end of a book needs your close attention because it usually is meant to wrap up all the little details and plot bits, explain what needs explanation, put a final exclamation point on the themes, leave the characters in a situation of equilibrium (noting what has happened to all the important characters), and send the reader off feeling that all loose ends have been tied up. The ending should make sense of the foreshadowings and plot development that have occurred in the book, and play out the main ideas that have been treated in the book.

It is true, however, that some authors are more explicit than others in wrapping things up, and some leave questions for the readers, either to infer the answers, or to show that things are just not that neat and tidy.

1. Write a postscript or extension for *The Giver* in which you answer the following questions:

    a. Did Jonas hear music or an echo behind him? In defense of whichever one you think, explain what happened in the community after Jonas left. Did things go at all as he and The Giver had planned?

    b. What happened to Jonas and Gabriel when they reached Elsewhere? Were there people there to meet them? Were they expected? What kind of society was it? What were people doing?

    c. Does any connection ever form between Elsewhere and the community from which Jonas and Gabriel came?

    d. What happens to The Giver?

    e. What are the roles Jonas and Gabriel will play in Elsewhere?

Name _____

Vocabulary

Look at each group of words. Tell why it is important in the story.

1. outlying, rutted, taut, vigilant _____

_____

2. jolted, wincing, gullies _____

_____

3. loomed, trudged, summit _____

_____

Essay Topics

1. If Jonas and The Giver's plan had worked, do you think the community would have sent out search planes? What does the presence of the planes suggest about what was happening back in the community?

2. In what ways are the memories that The Giver shared with Jonas different from memories you have? What do you think Lowry is saying about memories?

3. The Giver said (page 162), "My work will be finished . . . when I have helped the community to change and become whole. . . . When my work here is finished, I want to be with my daughter." What do you think of this? Do you think he got his desire or do you think his desire may have changed?

4. Do you think this book has a "happy" ending? Explain your response.

5. What part of the book is the most memorable for you? Explain what this part means to you.

6. Has this book changed any of your fundamental ideas? Explain your answer.

7. Create an illustration for your favorite part of the book. Write a paragraph explaining how your illustration depicts the section of text you have chosen.

8. Are you in any way a Giver or a Receiver? If you are, explain how. If you feel you are not, explain why not.

9. In your opinion, can community exist without shared memories and feelings? Explain your answer.

10. Do you think the title of the book was well chosen? Why or why not?

11. Was Jonas a good community member? Explain your response.

Strategy 1: Beginning a Book, pages 11–12

1. Answers will vary. Students may mention ideas and words that they associate with the concept of giving: presents, generosity, celebrations, appreciation. They may identify the term as a personal title meaning "the one who gives" and wonder about what kind of person would have a title like that.
2. Answers will vary and most likely relate to students' responses to #1 above.
3. Answers will vary. Students should refer both to the black-and-white photograph of an older man, whom they may identify with the title, and the color portion that shows a landscape with trees in the sunshine and snow on the ground. They may describe the man as troubled or sad. They should speculate on the relationship between the two photographs and the meaning of the torn edge. They might speculate on which picture is being torn to reveal the other. Students may note that the hard cover is red. Later they may connect this to the significance of red as the first color Jonas is able to see.
4. It was published in 1993.
5. Answers will vary.
6. It has won the Newbery Medal. Students' associations with this award will vary.
7. Possible response: The narrator seems precise and careful, and for this reason, trustworthy. The narrator has access to Jonas's inner thoughts and feelings, as well as general information about life and the world of the book.
8. Possible response: While it seems from the cover that the old man pictured and "The Giver" (possibly the same person) are the most important, it seems from the first 4 pages as if Jonas is very important.
9. It takes place in an unidentified community. It seems to be an imaginary setting. Answers will vary. The community seems to be run by a group of people who control all details of life. People depend on the government for everything, and it appears that uniformity is highly valued.
10. The lack of a community name and the type of government might lead students to identify this as science fiction or as a dystopia, if they happen to know the term.
11. Answers will vary. Given the attention paid to Jonas and the type of community, there might be a focus on the individual vs. the community.
12. Answers will vary. Students may predict that Jonas will come into conflict with the community in some way.
13. Answers will vary.

Chapter 1, page 12

1. Answers will vary. Students may focus on predictions about the content of the Ceremony of Twelve and what it will bring for Jonas's future. They may wonder what connection this has to The Giver.
2. Students may be puzzled by the idea of "release," which seems to be associated with punishment, honor, and expediency in getting rid of problems (newchildren who don't thrive), all in one. They may find that they like the society less and less.
3. Students may identify the use of capitalized job titles to replace names; of numbers instead of names for newchildren; of the lack of a proper name for the community or for Jonas's parents; the insistence on precision of language, coupled with the use of a universally understood word like *animal* without understanding; the reference to "a male" instead of "a boy" in Lily's explanation about what made her angry.
4. Students should note elements such as order, rules, control, power, dependence, uniformity, obedience. They should note the child-rearing methods; the family structure; the enforced sharing of feelings; the subservience to the loudspeaker; the lack of initiative in an "emergency;" etc.
5. It may reveal that he is a good student and follows the path that the community values, and/or it may show that he is a careful person who values precision.
6. Students may have positive feelings about sharing the day's events or negative feelings about enforced sharing of personal matters.
7. Students will likely be confused that one word encompasses the treatment of transgressors, unhealthy newchildren, and the elderly. They may suggest that it involves going to another place that is considered less desirable. Some may think that people being released are killed.

Strategy 2: Setting and Mood, page 14

In their use of the chart, students should show awareness of the various uses of setting. In the last chapters, they should note how the setting creates obstacles to the success of the escape attempt.

Strategy 3: Irony, page 15

Answers may vary. Here are some examples of irony that students might note in Chapter 19: the situational irony that part of Father's job as a Nurturer is to kill babies; the verbal irony in the way Father speaks to the twin that he releases (which only becomes apparent once we realize that he has killed it); the dramatic irony that suggests to the reader through the description of the injection and The Giver's manner as they watch, that Father is going to kill the baby, before Jonas realizes it.

Writer's Forum 1: Shades of Meaning, page 16

Students' rewritten paragraphs should demonstrate an understanding of the concept of shades of meaning. The analysis should include an accurate description of how their passage differs from Lowry's.

Chapter 2, page 17

1. Students will likely feel that both instances were justified. They may sense a disturbing gap between the apparent commitment to the welfare of the newchildren and the resistance to naming them. They may find it arbitrary and irrational to give bikes to Nines and forbid Eights to ride.
2. Students should mention such things as children staying in the family to which they are born; immediate naming; presence of family members at birth; family as nurturers. Students who are familiar with adoption may point to it as a choice, not a universal practice. They may be skeptical because it is implicitly suggested that in the community, these placements always work well.
3. Answers will vary. Students who are very sensitive to the mood of fear and paranoia evoked at the beginning of Chapter 1 and who feel strongly that the community is evil may expect breakdowns in relationships and lots of irony.
4. Answers will vary. Students should relate their predictions to Jonas's characteristics.
5. Answers will vary. Students may need to come to terms with the difference between how they might appear to others and what they are "actually" like.
6. He is the most important Elder and has final say in decisions. Other than that, it is not clear who he is or what he does.
7. The narrator is presenting the information from the characters' perspective, and apparently, they don't know what animals are (see page 5) and think that they are imaginary.
8. Students may enjoy the idea of such a large celebration or balk at the idea of not having an individual birthday party.

Writer's Forum 2: Anecdote, page 18

Students' anecdotes should be based on the content of the story, with details added as needed. They should have the characteristics of anecdotes, including brevity, humor if desired, etc.

Chapter 3, page 19

1. Answers will vary. Students may think that differences are not in and of themselves bad, and that they should be acknowledged as part of reality.
2. Focusing on a topic at the beginning of a book or chapter, at the end of a book or chapter, and more than once, are all ways an author has of drawing readers' attention to something important. Jonas's interpretation of the look that pale eyes give a person is also important. Lowry is encouraging readers to pay attention to this characteristic because it is important or symbolic of some deeper meaning.
3. Students may or may not find the use of all capital letters to convey the loud drone of the Speakers effective.
4. The text gives a clue when the apple is described as being a "nondescript shade," suggesting that there is no color in this world, but only very astute readers will realize that Jonas has seen color in a colorless world.

Strategy 4: Plot—The Design of a Story, page 20

Answers will vary. Possible response: The first 56 pages (into Chapter 7) make up the Exposition—introduction of essential background information, as well as characters, situations, and conflicts. You might say that the complication arises on page 57, when Jonas is separated out from his groupmates and the community. The crisis might be in Chapter 19, when Jonas realizes what his father has done and what happened to Rosemary, and must come to terms with what this means about the community. The result is that he and

The Giver make the plan that will determine the outcome of the story and the conflict. When Jonas finds the sled on page 179, all the pieces fall into place—this is the climax. The last two pages suggest that the conflicts are resolved, and the story is concluded—this is the resolution.

Chapter 4, page 21

1. Their lives seem to be regulated in every area except their volunteer hours and the recreation hours they are alloted before they become Twelves and begin training.
2. Students may agree that it is good to inhibit bragging, or they may feel that it is important to be able to talk about accomplishments in order to share information, share pleasure at a job well done, etc.
3. Students should notice that areas are described only by name, not by physical characteristics (such as color, shape, size, or equipment), or by explicit location. Students may note that the Auditorium does not seem to be closed in. This suggests that the community may exist in an enclosed environment in which the weather and climate are controlled.
4. He understands the various areas of the community and is aware of their differences, but he has no idea what his Assignment will be because he hasn't developed a focus for himself.
5. Possible response: They are bathed by others; they are peaceful; they can be seen naked by others; release for them is not a punishment.
6. Answers will vary. Students may think it means nothing more than that they have performed the Assignments the community gave them.
7. Students may continue to be confused about the conflicting views of release as celebration and punishment. They may, however, be suspicious of the closed door, the fact that nobody is allowed to see the actual moment of release.

Chapter 5, page 22

1. Students may feel that individuals should be able to decide for themselves whether or not to share their dreams.
2. Answers will vary. Students may speculate that meals are prepared elsewhere and then delivered to peoples' homes.
3. Wording will differ, but students should convey that Jonas experiences his first feelings of sexual attraction, and the pills suppress sexual desire.
4. Possible response: It is clear that the birth of children and the matching of couples are both carefully controlled; to maintain this control, people have to be prevented from having any experience of their own sexuality.

Strategy 5: Foreshadowing and Flashback, page 23

1. Answers will vary. Possible response: Jonas's recollection of the incident with the apple is a flashback.
2. Answers will vary. Possible response: The Giver's responses to Jonas in Chapter 19 signal that something unexpected and unpleasant will be revealed in the film of the release.

Writer's Forum 3: A List of Rules, page 24

Answers will vary depending on the community and activity.

Test 1: Chapters 1–5, page 25

Vocabulary
1. Jonas's taking the apple home and then disposing of it
2. Children choosing volunteer hours in preparation for their Assignments
3. Jonas's inability to understand what happened to the apple
4. Larissa

Essay Topics
1. Answers will vary.
2. Answers will vary depending on the story chosen.
3. Answers will vary depending on the story and character chosen.
4. Answers will vary.

5. Answers will vary.
6. Students' answers will vary depending on what they think happens when someone is released. Students may speculate that individual life is not valued, so people are maintained only when they provide something of value to the community.
7. Students may like the courtesy and lack of conflict. They may dislike the control, obedience, dependence, etc.
8. Students may reason that children of this age would like to start with something familiar or that they start with it because it is fun or it gives them an opportunity to be with younger children—perhaps a brother or sister.

Chapter 6, page 26

1. Students may think that it's unrealistic to promise that you won't become attached to a child who lives with you for a year. Very astute students may refer to the Ceremony of Release and the narrator's comment at the end of the passage about Caleb: "the little Four seemed to fade away gradually from everyone's consciousness," and posit that if a 1-day ceremony can blot out a child's existence, maybe the people in this community are so disengaged that they CAN promise not to become involved.
2. Because it would have ruined the perfect record of no releases for the year. Students may find it ironic because the values are misplaced: the record is valued more than the child.
3. Students may find it very strange to substitute one child for another.
4. Students may note the quick disappearance of the child from the consciousness of the community.
5. Students may feel that never seeing a person again is a tragedy, whatever you call the reason.
6. Students may think that the community is extremely harsh and that the impact of an individual on the community good is given too much weight.
7. Drawings will vary. Students should accurately portray whatever details of the Ceremony they choose to include.
8. Students will probably find it unlikely, because real people are very complex to begin with and when they grow and change it affects their relationships.
9. Students may or may not trust the Elders' selection.
10. Answers will vary.

Strategy 6: Characterization, page 27

1. Lowry uses very little physical description of characters or setting. Only some characters have names. So far in the book, there has been little character development. Readers have access to Jonas's thoughts.
2. Students may feel some removal from the unnamed characters.
3. Students may note that his interactions are hampered by his lack of control over language.
4. There haven't been any.
5. Father seems to have the deepest feelings and to be characterized by a strong commitment to newchildren, which gives him the courage to take risks to save Gabe. That the committee responds to his request suggests that he is held in high regard. He seems reasonable, patient, understanding, and affectionate with his children.

Chapter 7, page 28

1. Answers will vary. Students should include some of the following qualities in their characterization: intelligent, well-spoken, kind, organized, efficient, personable, thoughtful
2. Students may appreciate the courtesy shown.
3. Most students will likely think that the Assignments fit the candidates perfectly.
4. Possible responses: He has, as he himself thinks, done something wrong. He has spread himself around so much that he has not really settled—like Gabriel, he will be given an extra year before he is placed. There is something special about his Assignment, so it is saved for last. The Chief Elder made a mistake.

Strategy 7: Forming Hypotheses, page 29

1. Answers will vary. Students' hypotheses should be based on evidence and revised according to the new evidence provided in each chapter.

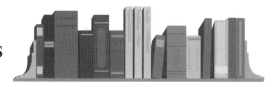

Chapter 8, page 30

1. He is "oddly separate" from the Committee, although he sits with them, and he has pale eyes.
2. Answers will vary. Perhaps he doesn't often appear in public; perhaps he is not very noticeable.
3. Asher's mother told him (page 48) that ten years before, someone had applied for release and was gone the next day. Students may speculate that the person who applied for release was the Receiver-in-Training.
4. The Committee must look for signs of qualities that are not yet present (like wisdom), and they have no ability to follow through with observations to make sure that their choice bears out.
5. Answers will vary. Students may think that this person is responsible for remembering the history of the community. They might compare this person to a historian, shaman, epic storyteller, or journalist.
6. Answers will vary but may include questions about the nature of being a Receiver, why there is pain involved, why solitude is necessary, whether light eyes have something to do with the selection, and what the Capacity to See Beyond is.

Strategy 8: Evaluating a Book, page 31

1. Evaluations will vary. Students should include the title, author, genre, and plot summary. Their judgments should be supported by evidence from the text and their reactions to it.

Chapter 9, page 32

1. Answers will vary. Students may think that Asher's lack of seriousness (page 17) will impede a serious and mature friendship, and that his hesitations (pages 65 and 66) foreshadow a distancing of the two.
2. Answers will vary. On the surface level, students may assume that she was released. They may guess that she broke the rules or turned out not to have the necessary qualities, such as seeing beyond, or couldn't stand the pain.
3. Answers will vary. Students may be struck overall by the amount of control exercised in Jonas's life, or they may be struck by a particular rule. Jonas is most struck by the rule about lying and the implication that others may have the same rule, leading him to wonder if he needs to re-evaluate everything.
4. Answers will vary. Students may conjecture that something about the role of Receiver makes casual contacts unnecessary or undesirable; that The Receiver's need for information outweighs the community commitment to politeness; that the special knowledge of The Receiver has to be protected; that The Receiver's dreams may have special meaning or importance; that the pain of the training must be borne and not eased for some reason; that The Receiver is too valuable to the community to be allowed to leave; that The Receiver's knowledge must be protected, even at the cost of imprecision.
5. Answers will vary. Students who have begun to suspect that the community is not as idyllic as it appears may think that others do lie, while students who have not yet begun to question the presentation of the community may not.

Strategy 9: Plot Conflict, page 33

1. Answers will vary. This book is unusual in that the major conflict a) develops later in the story than usual [students may identify either "I wish we had those things, still" (page 84) or "We shouldn't have" (page 95), as the first definitive statement of the conflict with the community] and b) involves multiple protagonists—Jonas, The Giver, and Gabriel. The conflict might be stated that the Giver and Receiver struggle to make the acts of giving and receiving memories universal in a community that, because it lacks memories, also lacks wisdom and feelings.

2. Because the beginning of the book provides background and reveals the gradual maturing of Jonas's view, the focus is more on Jonas's perspective than on conflict. Answers will vary.

Chapter	Conflict
1	Jonas's struggle to achieve precision of language
2	No clear conflict
3	Jonas's conflict with the rules because of his experience with the apple
4	No clear conflict
5	Jonas's desire in his dream, which he knows to be inappropriate, but pursues anyway

6	No clear conflict
7	The conflict within the community and especially within Jonas when Jonas is skipped at the Ceremony
8	Jonas's interior concern over what his selection means and whether he can fulfill the expectations
9	Jonas's reaction to his training rules
10	No clear conflict
11	Jonas's mild feeling of distress about Sameness; The Giver's ambivalence about transferring pain to Jonas
12	Jonas's inner conflict over the inadequacy of language; Jonas's anger against the community for choosing Sameness; The Giver's opposition to Sameness
13	Jonas's continued conflict with the unfairness of Sameness; Jonas's unspoken conflict with the community over his friends' and family's inability to receive memories; The Giver's conflict with the community over bearing the pain of the memories
14	Jonas and The Giver's seemingly unresolvable conflict with the community over bearing the pain of the memories instead of having the memories shared by all; Jonas's internal conflict over giving a memory to Gabriel without permission and over whether he should confess this transgression
15	Jonas and The Giver's struggle to bear the pain of the memory of warfare
16	Jonas's struggle with accepting his selection; Jonas's dissatisfaction with the lack of love in the community
17	Jonas's conflict with the community over the shallow emotions that pass for feelings; Jonas's conflict with his friends, particularly Asher, over their superficial understanding of the game of war
18	The Giver's conflict over having to give Rosemary painful memories; The Giver's conflict over his failure with Rosemary
19	Jonas and The Giver's conflict over release; Jonas's conflict with who his father is, the lies his father has told him, and the community that demands the lies
20	Jonas and The Giver's conflict over release continued; Jonas's conflict with who his father is and the lies his father has told him continued; Jonas's conflict over Fiona's training in release; Jonas and The Giver's conflict with Sameness and the role of Receiver of Memory; Jonas and The Giver's plan to elude the community's rules and force the memories back into the community
21	Jonas's flight to escape the community and evade capture; Jonas's conflict with his father and the community over Gabriel's scheduled release
22	Jonas's struggle to avoid starvation and freezing for himself and Gabriel
23	Jonas's struggle through the snow and cold to reach the summit of the hill

Chapter 10, page 34

1. Answers will vary. Students may suspect that, considering the esteem in which The Receiver is held, and the rules that permit him to be rude and lie, more than protecting his concentration is involved—they may think that there are some secrets being hidden.
2. The furnishings are chosen for beauty and quality, not just for function; there is a suggestion that his room may be larger than other rooms; he has far more than the three books found in every other dwelling.
3. Answers will vary. Possible responses include respectfully, gently, carefully, thoughtfully, as a colleague.
4. They are the "memories of the whole world," which lead to the wisdom that allows people to shape their futures.
5. That there are locked doors in the community; that the attendant shows him the respect of standing when he enters; the number of books the Receiver has; that the man doesn't use the community's standard response to an apology; that there exists something beyond the community and the current generation; the man's description of the weight of the memories; that the man has the power to turn off the speaker.
6. Answers will vary. Possible responses include: because they don't have them in his community.

Strategy 10: Point of View, page 35

1. No.
2. Answers will vary. There are many passages that convey what Jonas is thinking about, and which have no external expression.
3. No—only as thoughts and feelings are revealed to Jonas.
4. The narrator seems to be outside the events of the story.
5. The story is told from a limited third-person point of view.
6. Some examples of discourse that turn out to be ironic are the highly analytic discussion of feelings (pages 4–8) which is dissected in the story by Jonas on pages 131–132; Jonas's idea of asking his father if his father lies (page 71); Jonas's conception of the care and respect the Old receive in the House of the Old (page 123); Father's description of the Ceremony of Release for identical twins (page 137); Jonas's suggestion that Rosemary wasn't brave enough (page 142); Jonas's idea that the failure didn't seem so terrible (page 143); many of The Giver's comments from page 146 to 149; Jonas's characterization of Fiona (page 153)— This last example is revealed as ironic in the very next paragraph.

Writer's Forum 4, Description, page 36

1. Student's descriptions should include detailed information and be organized in a logical way. The note should point out the differences in the types of categories and in the organizational format used between the two essays.

Test 2: Chapters 6–10, page 37

Vocabulary

1. How the Committee observes Elevens while determining their Assignments.
2. Asher's use of language
3. The speech of the Chief Elder as she explains why she skipped Jonas
4. Jonas's selection as Receiver of Memory
5. Jonas's reflection on the rule about pain for the new Receiver of Memory
6. Description of the Receiver's room

Essay Topics

1. Answers will vary. Students may anticipate that the conflict will somehow involve the pain that Jonas has to face as Receiver, or some use of the wisdom he gains from the memories.
2. Answers will vary. Possible responses: Why can't everybody have the memories? What happened ten years before when the Receiver failed? Who is actually running the community and making the decisions?
3. The socially awkward moments with Asher and Fiona and the rules that Jonas must follow suggest that Jonas may become more and more separate from his friends.
4. Answers will vary. Students may refer to examples of political leaders who have lied; they may talk about lies in advertising; they may mention propaganda from leaders of cults and other organizations.
5. Answers will vary. Students may find Jonas immature and very dependent for his age, but still believe in him.
6. Answers will vary. Students may conclude that the community is someplace on earth, but that the particular spot is not important—only that the memories are connected to the history of human beings that we recognize.
7. Students may (now or later in their reading) identify the point of view as being a primary means of creating suspense—because Jonas is intelligent, perceptive, and precise, but initially has limited knowledge, the view through his eyes gradually expands. Therefore, the reader must wait for enlightenment until Jonas's experience or thought takes him to the next level of understanding. This approach allows the author to carefully control our reception of information. Because of techniques like foreshadowing and irony, we sometimes know more than Jonas, but we are limited by his point of view.
8. Answers will vary. Most students will probably like Jonas for qualities like his honesty, openness, vitality, intelligence, and eagerness.

Chapter 11, pages 38–39

1. Touch, taste, sight, and sound so far.
2. He has a double consciousness, both of his body on the bed and of the experience of the memory; he sees

with his eyes closed; the experience explains itself to him, giving him an understanding and even identifying the names of things he has never known before, but without verbal details.

3. Answers will vary. Accept reasonable answers.

4. In precise use of language, we can distinguish between receiving, which is more or less passively accepting what is offered, and taking, which suggests initiation or willful activity on the part of the actor.

5. Answers will vary. Possible response: They might have seen that uncontrolled elements, such as the weather, led to droughts and famines and death from freezing and starvation; and they might have seen that differences led to prejudice, racism, hatred, intolerance, and war, and hoped that Sameness would eradicate all these evils.

6. Answers will vary. Some students may think he does not speak unnecessarily; others may interpret his silence as indicating that Jonas's understanding is inadequate—that his ability to easily accept the pain of sunburn is—contrary to what Jonas believes—not a good indication of how he will respond to other types of pain.

7. Some students may think that he is recalling his first day with the female Receiver. Others may think that he is moved by Jonas's willingness to bear pain, but does not look forward to transmitting pain to him.

8. Students should mention devices such as publications (books, periodicals, etc.); storage facilities such as databases, archives, institutions of higher education, and libraries; techniques such as celebrations of traditions, rituals, storytelling; and people such as storytellers, teachers, grandparents, certain religious leaders.

9. Students may note that his role as Receiver of Memories is done, in that he is no longer acquiring memories from a trainer; rather, with the beginning of the training of Jonas, his focus is on giving the memories to the next Receiver. Students should link this name to the title, and may then leap to identifying the face on the cover. You may wish to come back to this idea and address it again when it becomes apparent later that Jonas is also a Giver.

10. Students may use adjectives such as intelligent, thoughtful, aloof, careful, gentle, sensitive.

Chapter 12, page 40–41

1. This is his first avoidance of a completely and precisely truthful communication.

2. Answers will vary. Some students may think that it is a foreshadowing of something that will develop later in the book. Some may think that it occurs simply because his mind is full of this new and striking experience.

3. He is discovering the limitations of language to convey experience (see pages 89 and 92).

4. Many students will not yet realize that color is involved, let alone the specific color red. They are likely to understand seeing beyond as seeing something beyond what they consider ordinary, and for them, ordinary will most likely already include color.

5. Answers will vary. Students may recognize that our understanding of historical sequence, and cause and effect would be marred or lost, and that enormous amounts of information that we consider fundamental would be unavailable.

6. Answers will vary. Students may grow more uneasy with Sameness as the extent of it is slowly revealed.

7. Answers will vary. Students may find it very difficult to think of any response.

8. He means that it took him many years to come to the conclusion that Jonas has already arrived at—that the community shouldn't have chosen Sameness.

9. He goes slowly and carefully, building on what Jonas already knows. He doesn't expect Jonas to have exactly the same experiences that he himself has had.

Chapter 13, pages 42–43

1. Because his perceptions and his role are different than those of not only his peers but all of his community except The Giver, his life cannot be considered ordinary.

2. Students may feel that The Giver's statement, "It's the choosing that's important, isn't it?" is consistent, but that his responses to Jonas's tentative exploration of what choice means ("He might make wrong choices"; "Not safe?"; Frightening, isn't it?"; "Much safer") tend to bolster the community's view and direct Jonas's thoughts away from the desire for choice and freedom.

3. Possible responses: He believes so strongly that it isn't fair that people can't choose, prompting him to try to find a way around the rules. He wants his friend to be able to share his perceptions. Possibly he would feel less alone.

4. On an emotional level, students may find it disturbing and/or moving. On an artistic level, they may appreciate the poignancy of the one elephant caring for and mourning the loss of the other, as a counterpoint to how casual the humans in the community are about losing someone through release.

5. Answers will vary. Students may make a connection between light eyes and the gift of being able to receive memories and have those perceptions.

6. Answers will vary. Students may be uncomfortable with a concept of family that ignores biology and a family life that is constructed only for the raising of children and then dismantled as soon as the children are grown.

7. Answers will vary. Students might gather that, because of his role in the community, The Giver sees his life as one of "being" rather than "doing." Or they might think that the task of bearing the memories is so difficult and all-consuming that nothing else has importance.

8. Possible response: People can only hear what they are ready to hear.

9. Possible response: Part of the meaning of our lives comes from the context provided by memory: we see how cause and effect work and we come to understand how our actions can change the world around us. Our relationships and decisions depend on memory. Our feelings and wisdom come from memories.

10. Possible responses: The honor is negligible compared to the pain and loneliness. The honor carries little practical power, because the role The Receiver might have is circumscribed by the community's lack of understanding.

11. Answers will vary. Students may picture this community as a last outpost of civilization (there is no Elsewhere), or as a ghetto of distorted ideals set on some island in the existing world (Elsewhere is the world as we know it).

12. Possible responses: thoughtfulness, courage, integrity, dedication, generosity, a true sense of community, trust.

Writer's Forum 5: Persuasion, page 44

1. Students' essays should counter Jonas's points about the cost of freedom with arguments and information that convincingly show that the benefits are worth the price.

Chapter 14, pages 45–46

1. Answers will vary. Possible response: Since pain is something that everyone in our world endures, our personal experience of pain can help make us sympathetic to the pain of others and understanding of the condition of people who in other ways are very unlike ourselves. It can also prompt us to shape our lives and our desires to help ourselves and others avoid unnecessary pain. For Jonas, pain does not connect him to others except The Giver (since no one else feels), but it does (or will) give him wisdom to plan well for the future.

2. Answers will vary. Students should provide support for their views. Some students may say that it depends: physical pain must, of necessity, be born more by individuals; sometimes sharing pain is more harmful than helpful.

3. Answers will vary. Students may recall the release of the female Receiver-in-Training and conjecture that there is at least a possibility of forcing the memories back to the people if Jonas and/or The Giver is willing to be released in order to do so.

4. Answers will vary. Students should support their answers.

5. Some students may already have realized that release is a euphemism for killing anyone who is not considered serviceable to the community. Others may believe that people who are released are sent to another place and live there.

6. Answers will vary. Students may wonder why Larissa couldn't remain in the community any longer, especially since there is a special place to care for the Old.

7. Possible responses: Perhaps he felt in some way that Gabriel had "taken" the memory, since he had made no conscious decision to "give" it. Perhaps he was simply surprised because it was the first time it had happened.

8. Gabriel's ability to receive may be connected with his light eyes.

9. Students may not find any clear indication of why Jonas does not trust The Giver with this information. They may imagine that he is afraid of the consequences.

Answer Pages

Strategy 11: Characterization Continuum, page 47

1. •*Gullible:* Students should recognize that because the community controls their schedules, their lives, and available information, all members of the community who are not in positions of power are gullible, especially children. Of course, this includes Jonas. Because Jonas is perceptive, because he comes into contact with the one person in the community who can and will speak the truth (The Giver), and because he is given access to the memories, he is able to attain understanding, insight, and wisdom. The book does not reveal whether the community will attain insight, but it is implied at the end that this will (or may) happen.

   •*Honest:* Students should recognize that Jonas's change from scrupulous honesty in accord with precision of language to being willing to lie and deceive is not simply a change from honesty to dishonesty. Jonas believes that his deceptions are serving a higher end (e.g. the things he does to save Gabriel from being killed). At the same time, there is a traceable sequence, from avoidance (page 88), to equivocation (page 110), to a full-fledged lie (page 127), to a planned and fully conscious concealed rejection of the community and all it stands for (pages 165–166).

   •*Follower/Dependent:* Students should realize that in some ways, The Giver is dependent and a follower in the community until Jonas urges him to break free. They should see that Jonas increases in independence and leadership until he is willing to sacrifice himself for the community and for Gabriel. They should see that Father is not merely dependent—if not for him, Gabriel would have died much sooner, when Jonas had no chance to save him, but Father's initiative takes place in a very limited sphere, and is not informed by true feelings and wisdom.

2. Answers will vary depending on the characters students choose. Students should use the categories in Strategy 6 as they discuss how character is revealed.

Chapter 15, page 48

1. He begins to give memories to Gabriel in Chapter 14, and he gives The Giver relief-from-pain of a different kind than that given by the community—by willingly sharing the painful memories with him.

2. Answers will vary. Students may think that dreadful memories can sometimes become bearable just by being shared; moreover, when we know each other's sufferings, we can offer real comfort instead of the shallow community version (see pages 4–9).

3. Students may say no, because Jonas offers his help or yes, because they feel that Jonas cannot possibly know what he's in for and so his offer to help was made in ignorance, while The Giver knew how much it would hurt and could have protected him. Students' responses to The Giver and their reasons for them will vary.

4. Students may predict that Jonas will be too scared of the pain to want to go back, or too angry (with The Giver and/or the community).

Writer's Forum 6: Diary Entries, page 49

1. Answers will vary. Entries should show consistent characterization and be recognizable as belonging to the character the student has identified.

Test 3: Chapters 11–15, page 50

Vocabulary

1. Jonas's experience of the first transmitted memory of a sled ride in the snow
2. Fiona's recounting of what she is learning in training at the House of the Old
3. Jonas's experience of the memory of the ivory hunters killing the elephant
4. Jonas's experience of the memory of hunger
5. The memory that Jonas, at first unwittingly, transmits to Gabriel
6. Jonas's experience of the memory of warfare

Essay Topics

1. Answers will vary.
2. Answers will vary. Students should follow some threads in the plot, possibly creating a scenario in which the memories are returned to their original state in which everyone shares them, or an attempt is made to return the memories, but the attempt fails.

3. Students should refer to the capitalization of job titles and their use in place of names as showing the importance of jobs in this community, and the subsuming of individuality. The titles of The Giver and The Receiver are further distinguished by having the definite article capitalized. This emphasizes the importance of these jobs beyond all the others and points to the fact that there is only one person to play each of these roles at any particular moment.
4. Possible response: Not only do the memories and feelings, which only Jonas and The Giver experience, set him apart from his friends, but he cannot even share them by discussing them, and this probably makes him feel very isolated and lonely.
5. Answers will vary. Students should support their opinions.
6. Students will have different ways of defining their lives.
7. Students may argue either for protecting children from horrors, or for helping children to acknowledge and face the truth.

Chapter 16, pages 51–52
1. The text says he doesn't have a choice. Students may interpret this to mean that in his society, there is no place to hide and no way of concealing his absence were he to miss a training.
2. It captures for him the joy of diversity and difference that is missing in his community.
3. Students may mention some or all of the following: lots of people, fire in the fireplace, nighttime, snow, colored lights on a tree in the house, candles, dinner, packages, unwrapping gifts. Most students will be sure as soon as the tree and lights are mentioned that the holiday is Christmas.
4. Students may judge the family scene in the home more favorably.
5. Since he doesn't repeat Jonas's words exactly, the omission could be significant. He may be giving a minimal agreement: agreeing that it works, but suggesting that "pretty well" is an exaggeration, or maybe even not true.
6. Students' responses will depend on what aspects of the scene they think Jonas found to be dangerous besides the fire; possibly he thinks that the Old will not get appropriate care if they are left to their families.
7. Possible response: He sees the impossibility of explaining his position, but also sees the futility of saying that his opinion is different. His solution is to pretend that he agrees. He sees that precision of language is limited by lack of understanding.
8. Students should mention change in areas such as maturity, independence, depth of feeling, compassion, love, sound judgment, honesty.
9. Answers will vary. While students may note that Gabriel cannot understand Jonas's words (both because he is too young and because Gabriel is asleep), Gabriel's light eyes and receptivity to receiving memory suggest that he will one day have the capacity to understand Jonas's position and to love. It is possible that Jonas is speaking to this potential in Gabriel.
10. Answers will vary. Possible response: The pills are part of the community's way of suppressing natural feelings. It is better to live with feelings, even if they are sometimes unwelcome or awkward, and learn to deal with them.

Writer's Forum 7: Personal Letter, page 53
1. Answers will vary. Students may mention that it is feelings, such as love, that help us to truly care for each other as friends, as family, and as members of the same community, even beyond the time when we "need" each other, and these feelings also help us give true respect and dignity to the Old.

Chapter 17, page 54
1. Students may have recognized the loudspeaker voice from the capital letters, used earlier to represent the announcement on page 23, or they may have recognized it from reading the attribution in the third line on page 130.
2. The depth of his feelings has increased; he now has colors to keep; he believes in an Elsewhere; he feels the need to reinterpret his past experience in the light of the memories and the knowledge and insight gained from them.
3. It marks a definitive separation from the group of children about his age, and in particular, from Fiona and Asher, who were his friends.

4. Answers will vary. Possible responses: He is too upset to want company. He realizes that the gulf between them is unbridgeable and attempting to bridge it would just make them both uncomfortable and unhappy.
5. Births must be induced, rather than allowed to occur naturally.
6. Students' responses will vary depending on how they interpret release at this time.

Strategy 12: Inferencing, page 55

1. Jonas probably realizes that Asher has no idea what "the past" is (last line, page 134) just as Jonas couldn't understand it before having memories; that without the memories, things don't have meaning (page 105); and that Asher is obviously impatient and unwilling to listen.
2. In addition to the factors mentioned in #1 above, Jonas probably is aware that further training will increasingly separate him from his friends, and he knows that this free time for recreation will not be readily available again.
3. Answers will vary. Some students may reason from the fact that there's another 40 pages to the book and from their previous experience of story lines, that the plot has to go somewhere and that there must be something Jonas has overlooked. Some students may recall the consequences of the loss of the last Receiver-in-Training and think that there are possibilities for change if Jonas and/or The Giver leave the community.

Chapter 18, page 56

1. Father had mentioned the release of the twin that was going to occur that day.
2. Possible response: The training for precise language and manners was so intense that Jonas has still not been able to overcome the habit of apologizing.
3. Possible response: It is a way of keeping himself going, of convincing himself that it is worthwhile, despite the pain and suffering and isolation.
4. The Giver tells Jonas that he loves him. He apologizes after transferring the memory of pain. The times The Giver has shown patience, concern, thoughtfulness, and kindness to Jonas show a depth of feeling for him. Mother and Father appreciate Jonas, but their feelings seem inadequate and diminished from what might be expected of parents. They deny that the word *love* has meaning, avowing that they enjoy and are proud of him, and apparently thinking that this is the most one could want.
5. Answers will vary. Jonas is able to imagine the scene. It is possible that The Giver's feelings are so strong that Jonas can capture them and bring them to life in his mind, or it may be that Jonas no longer needs the hands on his back to transfer a memory—he may be receiving the memory from The Giver's words alone.
6. The Giver is asking either for Jonas's understanding or for his forgiveness or approval.
7. Answers will vary depending on how students interpret the statement. They may interpret it as meaning that memories have an endurance beyond a human lifetime.
8. Possible response: He is thinking that there is a way that they can change things—but at the cost of Jonas leaving the community, which would entail enormous risks.

Chapter 19, page 57

1. Answers will vary depending on students' views of release. Possible responses: He wishes they wouldn't release an identical twin as a matter of course. He thinks that both twins could be of benefit to the community. OR, He thinks it's wrong to kill children, even though there are more born than the community planned for.
2. Students may think that it's clearly an insufficient reason for release, in whatever terms they currently understand release.
3. Possible responses: It's the word Jonas's father uses, so it made me think of him, and how much gentleness and concern he shows for Gabriel. It sounds much more warm and snugly than the word *comfortable* does. It's very ironic that Father talks so sweetly when he's planning to kill the baby, and when Jonas echoed this talk, it made me angry because the whole community is pretending that everything's perfect when actually they kill any babies and old people and "criminals" that they don't want around.
4. Answers may vary. Students who have inferred that release is a euphemism for killing may realize that The Giver knows this and that he thinks that Jonas needs to know it, too.
5. Students should sense irony in both sentences now.

6. Students' answers may include the following: The Giver's statements throughout the chapter, including the italicized ones: "I wish they wouldn't do that,"; *"Do you want to see this morning's release?"*; "I think you should"; "Shhh"; "Watch"; "Be quiet, Jonas . . . *Watch*"; "Shhh"; and the adverbs/adverbial phrases accompanying them: *firmly, in a strange voice, sharply.* Prior to this chapter, possible answers include the privacy of the release ceremonies for newchildren; Jonas's point that none of his group actually knows of a person who has joined another community (page 48—this doesn't fit with his idealized conception of newchildren going Elsewhere); the totalitarian nature of the community; the control and discipline wands for the Old.

7. Answers will vary. Some students may have realized prior to this chapter; others may be as surprised as Jonas. The clues they mention should support their conclusions about release.

8. He is clearly horrified by the idea of release, and he may also feel guilty or uneasy at his own easy dismissal of Rosemary's fate and at having questioned her courage.

9. Answers will vary. Accept reasonable responses.

10. Students' predictions will vary. They should be based on the known information about Jonas's character and the community.

Strategy 13: Rereading a Book, pages 58–59

1. Ironic elements include
   • page 146: Jonas's "chuckling" about the necessity of release; Jonas's enjoyment of the imaginary scene of release he has created in his mind based on his father's description; Jonas's assumption that privacy is the reason that watching a release is restricted
   • page 147: Jonas's indifference (shown by his shrugging) about whether or not he watches a release; Jonas's fear of watching a release centering around the privacy issue; Jonas's being "astonished and delighted" that he can watch the release
   • page 148: Jonas's innocent attention to the details of the setting as he tries to fit them in with the stories he's been told about the release of the Old; Father's saying that they'd "have a problem" if the twins weighed the same, as if killing the baby is not a problem but having to decide which one to kill would be
   • pages 148–149: The difference between life and death for one child being a matter of weighing six ounces less than the other
   • page 149: Jonas's comparison of the voice his father uses with the child he is about to kill to the voice he uses with Gabriel; Jonas's prediction regarding what his father will do next based on what his father told him; Jonas's special curiosity about the "ceremony part"; Jonas's sympathy in connecting the syringe to injections he's received to insure his health
   • page 150: Jonas's continued assumption that the "clean and comfy" part is coming; Jonas's inability to recognize death except from the memory, because no one except those who are trained to kill sees death in the community; Father's matter of fact performance of the proper procedures of clean-up after killing another human being
   • page 151: Father's putting the baby's body in the trash; Father's light-hearted farewell to the child he killed; the reiteration of Jonas's suggestion that Rosemary wasn't brave

   Answers regarding which of the ironic passages were identified only upon rereading will vary depending on when students noticed the ironies

Chapter 20, pages 60–61

1. Possible response: Having no memories and no feelings, the people who kill have never received what they need to treat other lives with the respect they deserve. Because they have not been given these keys to understanding, they cannot (on some level) be held responsible for their actions.

2. Students' expressions may include blame for those who turned a gentle, sensitive girl into a killer.

3. Students will probably be convinced that sharing memories is necessary to understanding and living with respect for others.

4. He is referring to The Giver's idea expressed on the bottom of page 144.

5. Pale eyes are THE signal of a person who has the qualities and abilities that make him or her capable of receiving and giving memories and attaining the wisdom and understanding that the memories bring. The links to the pale eyes of Jonas, The Giver, Gabriel, and Katharine with those attributes show that this is the connection.

6. Possible response: In a weak moment, longing for the company of the one adult in the community who loves him, Jonas says something he knows is not true in what he realizes is a vain attempt to convince The Giver to go with him. He hangs his head because he is ashamed of having said something unworthy of his understanding and unworthy of The Giver.
7. Most students will express sympathy with his loss.
8. Answers will vary. Some students may feel that Jonas has lost integrity in some way, even though the rules give him permission to lie. Most will likely feel that deception is necessary in this situation in order to bring about change and to prevent Jonas from being "released," which they may feel he would be if he expressed his true views. His ability to lie "easily" may allow him to give humanity back to the community.
9. Because he will not have school, he can go out before his parents wake in the morning and seem only inconsiderate, not criminal; because it would reflect on their parenting, his parents will not tell others of his absence; because his family must appear at the Ceremony, they will not look for him; because people in training no longer necessarily sit with their age group, his friends will assume he's with his family or The Giver, whereas his family will guess that he's joined up with his friend—it will be a long while before anyone realizes that Jonas isn't there; searchers will not go out before midday, and will then find the bicycle and clothing, which no one else will have disturbed or found; the people will already be assembled, so The Giver will be able to begin the Ceremony of Loss and deal with the onslaught of memories immediately.
10. Answers will vary. Students may say they were moved, or say that it's poignant that Jonas finds someone who loves him and then must leave forever.
11. This knowledge requires a reinterpretation of most of the material from Chapter 18 on. It not only adds depth and meaning to the story of the failure, but will cause review of the character of The Giver, who may appear to be heroic or horrible to students when they understand that the man who gave Rosemary loneliness and pain was her father. It becomes more apparent why Rosemary trusted The Giver so much and was eager to learn, and why she kissed him before she left to apply for release.

Writer's Forum 8: Reflection, page 62
1. Students' reflections should include their personal responses to the prompts listed and reveal an understanding of the impact of what Jonas has seen on his understanding of both his past and his future.

Strategy 14: Theme, page 63
1. Answers will vary. Students will likely focus on memory, love, community, family, feelings. They may also discuss the meaning of life and death, change, sacrifice, choices, belonging, sameness and diversity, society, responsibility, the individual and the system, and freedom.

Writer's Forum 9: Essay, page 64
1. Students' essays will vary depending on the theme or themes they choose to discuss.

Test 4: Chapters 16–20, page 65
Vocabulary
1. Jonas's reaction to the memory of love
2. Children's postures in the game of war
3. The Giver's experience in training Rosemary
4. Father's killing of the smaller of the two identical twins
5. The Giver's taking the stage to lead the community in the Ceremony of Loss after the announcement of Jonas's "death"

Essay Topics
1. Answers will vary. Students may see them as high points in their year and feel that a group celebration would be meaningless.
2. Students may substitute other memories of togetherness and sharing—different religious holy days, such as Hanukkah, Kwanzaa, Easter, First Communion, Confirmation, Bar or Bat Mitzvah; family celebrations such as Thanksgiving, Mother's Day, Father's Day, birthdays, or weddings. Other possibilities include the return home of someone who has been recovering in the hospital from an illness or injury; the return home of someone who has been gone for a long time or on a long or arduous journey; the birth of a child.

3. There is reason to expect him to have the same qualities that The Giver and Jonas have.
4. Possible areas of contrast are adoption is carried out using a different system; adoption is not the only option—most people keep their biological children; adoption is for life—it's not a relationship that ends when children become adults.
5. Answers will vary. Possible responses include the following: She couldn't bear the pain. She couldn't stand to receive the painful memories from her father. She saw how much it hurt her father to give her painful memories, and she knew it would only get worse, so she decided to spare him. She realized how misguided the restriction of memories was and refused to be a part of such a dehumanizing practice.
6. Possible response: He learned to be more thoughtful in his training methods. He found ways to protect Jonas and ease him along. Perhaps most important, he grew more aware of the horrors of the system, so that when Jonas came along, the groundwork was laid for The Giver to have the idea that might lead them all back to humanity and freedom.
7. It seems clear that the black and white image is The Giver. Other answers will vary. Possible response: The image behind The Giver, seen through a tear in the black and white photograph, could be a *memory* of the world when there was sunshine and color or an image of the world that will be *restored* due to The Giver and Jonas's efforts. The tactile difference in the pictures may possibly be interpreted as follows: the noticeably "shiny" feel of the colored photograph is a hint of the heightened sensations in that world as opposed to the "duller" feel of the black and white world of the community.

Chapter 21, pages 66–67
1. Answers will vary. Students may imagine that the plan was discovered; that Jonas or The Giver got sick or hurt; that some arrangement was made by the community that would change the organization of the Ceremony in a way that made the escape impossible; that the borders were closed.
2. Answers will vary. Accept reasonable answers.
3. The necessary silence of the escape with Jonas's silent communication to The Giver contrasts with the emphasis on the sounds of "normal" communication involved at dinnertime: *chattering, comments, babbling.*
4. Students may find the callousness with which Father announces Gabe's impending release and the matter-of-fact way in which Lily and Mother respond unbelievable or horrifying. Upon reading of the plan to release Gabe, students will be able to infer why Jonas was forced to flee.
5. So he could save him.
6. Answers will vary. Students may wonder why Father bothered to break the rules for Gabe in the first place. They may have a fuller understanding of how little feeling the members of the community have and how detached they are. Some students may look at how much potential Father has— considering that he still would take the trouble to try to nurture Gabe when he didn't have the support and benefit of the memories and accompanying feelings, wisdom, etc.—and be disturbed about what the community has "done to" him.
7. Possible response: In the beginning of the book, Jonas trusts the decisions and traditions of his community and views it as protective and capable. He is dependent on the community and sees it from a child's perspective. Now, having received memories that show him other possibilities for life, and having chosen to be independent of the community, he has the ability to take an analytic look at it. Recognizing the cost of the order and discipline the community has attained, he rejects the community's ways.
8. Possible response: In a situation in which there was little food available, unfair distribution of food could have serious results for the community/family/individuals. If someone took leftovers, it could be a serious matter because health, or even life, might be at stake.
9. Answers will vary. Students may speculate that Jonas's parents searched for him themselves, but without revealing his absence to others at first; that his absence from school was reported; that The Giver was questioned; that a search was mounted for Jonas and Gabriel; that people panicked, recalling the last time a Receiver-in-Training was lost; that preparations were made for the return of the memories to the people.
10. Answers will vary. Possible responses: Maybe they had assimilated the memories, so they didn't need Jonas back anymore. Maybe, since the damage was done, they didn't want to spend anymore time and energy looking for him.

Answer Pages

Strategy 15: Narration, p. 68

1. Answers will vary. Possible response: The last thought Jonas has that is unreliable is "he had made a wrong choice" (page 174). After that, everything is reliable, and it has to be, because for us to believe in the ending of a book narrated from a limited third-person point of view from Jonas's perspective, we must find Jonas trustworthy. Otherwise, we could understand the end as Jonas's fantasy as he lies dying in the snow, or as a hallucination or a dream. The groundwork for this trust in Jonas was laid with his careful use of language, mentioned on page 1, his foreknowledge that there would be a destination (page 88), and the fact that he recognizes the lights shining from inside the house as being like those in the memory of love at Christmas time.

Chapter 22, page 69

1. Squirrel.
2. Fear of the unknown peril and exquisite happiness.
3. Answers will vary. Students may point out that the memories were (presumably) still released, so the community may be returning to a life of feeling and understanding making the sacrifice worthwhile.
4. Possible response: Overcome with hunger and fear, Jonas again (as on page 156) has an unworthy thought, but is very quickly recalled to his higher principles when he thinks of what the alternative would have meant to Gabriel.
5. Possible response: Jonas was willing to take enormous risks to restore the community, but he took even greater risks to save Gabriel. To have that fail, to fail the one person left for him to love, might seem far more unbearable than losing his own life, the possibility of which he accepted when he agreed to leave the community.
6. Answers will vary. Students who recall Jonas's dream (page 88) and Jonas's and The Giver's certainty that Elsewhere exists (page 158) may predict that he will reach Elsewhere. Some students may think that we will find out that Jonas has saved the community, but that it will be at the cost of his and Gabriel's lives.

Chapter 23, page 70

1. Students may report moments of intuition or insight that were not supported by "sensory data."
2. Answers will vary. Students may think that they can do nothing and will die, or that they will press on and find Elsewhere.
3. Jonas is The Giver and Gabriel is The Receiver. Possibly Gabriel will grow up to be a Giver, too (we don't know how things work Elsewhere) or perhaps in Elsewhere all people are Givers AND Receivers.
4. Instead of trying to bring up and share memories given to him by The Giver, he begins to be filled with his own memories of his own life.
5. Possible response: The memories given by The Giver and Jonas's dreams of Elsewhere have merged and become a single reality.
6. Possible responses: A world where people are joined together, celebrating Christmas and family and love. An ideal version of our world of democracy and freedom and interdependence.
7. Answers will vary. Accept reasonable responses.

Strategy 16: Dystopias, page 71

1. Possible response: Because it shows a dehumanized society, and criticizes our society's struggle to deal with the issues attending what is sometimes called euthanasia, *The Giver* is a dystopia.
2. Possible response: Yes, Lowry is addressing euthanasia (so-called) and possibly abortion, and any attitudes that do not value the dignity of human life, young and old. She may also be criticizing the attitude that says that information access is the fundamental core of education, by emphasizing the importance of memory and understanding and feeling, all of which contribute to how we deal with information and make decisions.
3. Answers will vary. Students may feel that the book is simply a story or they may feel that there is a persuasive element as Lowry tries to convince readers to value memories and history. In an age when some people claim that the Holocaust did not really happen and students may not be learning about it, the importance of memory and history in preventing a recurrence of genocide in the world may be a point she wishes to emphasize.

Answer Pages

Writer's Forum 10: Extending a Story, page 72

1. Answers will vary. Students may address the points directly or indirectly and in any order. The plot and characterization should be reasonable extensions of Lowry's presentation.

Test 5: Chapters 21–23, page 73

Vocabulary

1. The escape from the community
2. The perils of the unfamiliar landscape as Jonas and Gabriel get farther away from the community
3. The mountain on which the sled is awaiting them

Essay Topics

1. The point of the bicycle and clothes by the river was to give the impression of Jonas's death and prevent a search, so the answer would be no. Possible response: They are terrified by the onslaught of memories and hope to bring Jonas back to contain them.
2. Possible responses include the level of reality that is experienced when recalling a memory: we don't really feel the pain of injury with the memory of injury, or feel cold with the memory of coldness. We cannot share memories with each other as completely as The Giver and Jonas do. Lowry may be suggesting that memories have enormous power, or just emphasizing how closely they connect us with the past and with each other.
3. Answers will vary. Lowry does not deal with the topic of an afterlife, but students may bring it up. "If memories are forever, are people forever, too?" is a question they may choose to address. It's possible that if the plan works and the memories are shared, all members of the community will become Givers and Receivers. If this were the case, perhaps The Giver would feel differently about leaving. In any case, students may point out, it would be unlikely that release would still be an option.
4. If students think the music was from the community, they may say yes. If they think it was just an echo, they may think that the community was not saved, so they may say no, because Jonas and The Giver's plan failed. Or they may say yes, simply because they believe Jonas and Gabriel found a true home, with welcome and love, and that is enough.
5. Answers will vary. Students should support their answers.
6. Answers will vary. Students should support their answers.
7. Illustrations will vary.
8. Students may discuss sharing memories or experiences with others and what this means in their lives.
9. Students may be convinced that shared memories and feelings are essential to community.
10. Answers will vary. Students should support their answers.
11. Answers will vary depending on whether students define a good community member as one who most perfectly embodies the ideals of the community or one who does what is in the community's best interest—whether or not the community recognizes its own best interest.

ENGLISH SERIES

The **Straight Forward English** series is designed to measure, teach, review, and master specific English skills. All pages are reproducible and include answers to exercises and tests.

Capitalization & Punctuation
GP-032 • 40 pages

I and First Words; Proper Nouns; Ending Marks and Sentences; Commas; Apostrophes; Quotation Marks.

Nouns & Pronouns
GP-033 • 40 pages

Singular and Plural Nouns; Common and Proper Nouns; Concrete and Abstract Nouns; Collective Nouns; Possessive Pronouns; Pronouns and Contractions; Subject and Object Pronouns.

Verbs
GP-034 • 40 pages

Action Verbs; Linking Verbs; Verb Tense; Subject-Verb Agreement; Spelling Rules for Tense; Helping Verbs; Irregular Verbs; Past Participles.

Sentences
GP-041 • 40 pages

Sentences; Subject and Predicate; Sentence Structures.

Adjectives & Adverbs
GP-035 • 40 pages

Proper Adjectives; Articles; Demonstrative Adjectives; Comparative Adjectives; Special Adjectives: Good and Bad; -ly Adverbs; Comparative Adverbs; Good-Well and Bad-Badly.

Prepositions, Conjunctions and Interjections
GP-043 • 40 pages

Recognizing Prepositions; Object of the Preposition; Prepositional Phrases; Prepositional Phrases as Adjectives and Adverbs; Faulty Reference; Coordinating, Correlative and Subordinate Conjunctions.

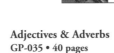

ADVANCED ENGLISH SERIES

Get It Right!
GP-148 • 144 pages

Organized into four sections, **Get It Right!** is designed to teach writing skills commonly addressed in the standardized testing in the early grades: Spelling, Mechanics, Usage, and Proofreading. Overall the book includes 100 lessons, plus reviews and skill checks.

All-In-One English
GP-107 • 112 pages

The **All-In-One** is a master book to the Straight Forward English Series.
Under one cover it has included the important English skills of capitalization, punctuation, and all eight parts of speech. Each selection of the All-In-One explains and models a skill and then provides focused practice, periodic review, and testing to help measure acquired skills. Progress through all skills is thorough and complete.

Grammar Rules!
GP-102 • 250 pages

Grammar Rules! is a straightforward approach to basic English grammar and English writing skills. Forty units each composed of four lessons for a total of 160 lessons, plus review, skill checks, and answers. Units build skills with Parts of Speech, Mechanics, Diagramming, and Proofreading. Solid grammar and writing skills are explained, modeled, practiced, reviewed, and tested.

Clauses & Phrases
GP-055 • 80 pages

Adverb, Adjective and Noun Clauses; Gerund, Participial and Infinitive Verbals; Gerund, Participial, Infinitive, Prepositional and Appositive Phrases.

Mechanics
GP-056 • 80 pages

Abbreviations; Apostrophes; Capitalization; Italics; Quotation Marks; Numbers; Commas; Semicolons; Colons; Hyphens; Parentheses; Dashes; Brackets; Ellipses; Slashes.

Grammar & Diagramming Sentences
GP-075 • 110 pages

The Basics; Diagramming Rules and Patterns; Nouns and Pronouns; Verbs; Modifiers; Prepositions, Conjunctions, and Special Items; Clauses and Compound-Complex Sentences.

Troublesome Grammar
GP-019 • 120 pages •

Agreement; Regular and Irregular Verbs; Modifiers; Prepositions and Case, Possessives and Contractions; Plurals; Active and Passive Voice; Comparative Forms; Word Usage; and more.

Math Series

The Straight Forward Math Series

is systematic, first diagnosing skill levels, then *practice*, periodic *review*, and *testing*.

Blackline

GP-006 Addition
GP-012 Subtraction
GP-007 Multiplication
GP-013 Division
GP-039 Fractions
GP-083 Word Problems, Book 1
GP-042 Word Problems, Book 2

The Advanced Straight Forward Math Series

is a higher level system to diagnose, practice, review, and test skills.

Blackline

GP-015 Advanced Addition
GP-016 Advanced Subtraction
GP-017 Advanced Multiplication
GP-018 Advanced Division
GP-020 Advanced Decimals
GP-021 Advanced Fractions
GP-044 Mastery Tests
GP-025 Percent
GP-028 Pre-Algebra, Book 1
GP-029 Pre-Algebra, Book 2
GP-030 Pre-Geometry, Book 1
GP-031 Pre-Geometry, Book 2
GP-163 Pre-Algebra Companion

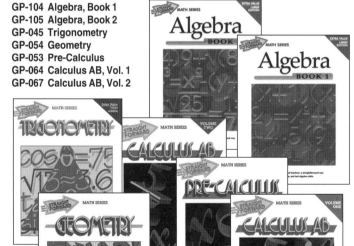

Upper Level Math Series

GP-104 Algebra, Book 1
GP-105 Algebra, Book 2
GP-045 Trigonometry
GP-054 Geometry
GP-053 Pre-Calculus
GP-064 Calculus AB, Vol. 1
GP-067 Calculus AB, Vol. 2

Math Pyramid Puzzles

Math Pyramid Puzzles
ISBN 978-1-9308-2062-3
GP-162
5 two-sided puzzles

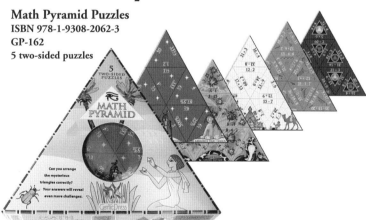

Assemble 5 two-sided puzzles each with different mathematical challenges. Solve the mathematical pyramid on the front side, turn the clear tray over to reveal of problem of logic: percents, decimals, fractions, exponents and factors.

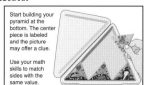

Start building your pyramid at the bottom. The center piece is labeled and the picture may offer a clue.

Use your math skills to match sides with the same value.

You may find more than one match, but **all sides that touch** must match. When you are satisfied with your solution, close the tray.

Turn over and check the back. If the pieces are in order, you are correct!

Now, can you solve this logic puzzle?